A Country Dweller's Years

Kesson revisits Proctor's Orphan Training Home in July 1988 (courtesy of Alistair Scott)

A Country Dweller's Years
Nature Writings By
Jessie Kesson

Edited with an Introduction by
Isobel Murray

Kennedy & Boyd

Kennedy & Boyd
an imprint of
Zeticula
57 St Vincent Crescent
Glasgow
G3 8NQ
Scotland.

http://www.kennedyandboyd.co.uk
admin@kennedyandboyd.co.uk

ISBN-13 978-1-904999-96-6 Paperback
ISBN-10   1-904999-96-4 Paperback

Contents

A school photo from Skene Central, c. 1928. Jessie is at the centre of the photograph (courtesy of Avril Wilbourne)

List of Illustrations

Kesson at the cottar house in Udale, where the film of Another Time, Another Place *was filmed, and which is remembered in 'Highland Spring'. (courtesy of Alistair Scott)*

Introduction

Jessie Kesson's early story is quite well known, but little has been published about her later life in Scotland, and her early writing career. This introduction aims to focus on these years, indicating the difficulties the writer faced, and the volume contents are more or less the product of this time. First, a cross-section of Jessie Kesson's young life, the year 1946, when Jessie was twenty-nine, and turned thirty. As well as this I want to stress the importance of one particular theme in her work, a passionate response to the natural world.

So for now we will pass over the Inverness workhouse where Kesson was born, the Corporation Lodging House in Elgin and the slum at Lady's Lane, her removal from a neglectful but much loved mother, the orphanage at Skene, the Aberdeen Hostel for Girls on Probation, the terrible teenage year in mental hospital at Cornhill in Aberdeen, the time she spent boarded out as a patient in Abriachan above Loch Ness, her courtship and marriage with Johnny Kesson. We ignore too the short residence in Aberdeen where baby Avril was born when Kesson was twenty-two, and the happy prewar interlude on Skye, broken when Johnny's road building occupation halted with the outbreak of war. The Kessons began their twelve or so years of operating as cottar farm workers, mostly in the north east, 1939-1951.

Kesson was determined to write. In 1941 she began publishing in *North-East Review* and the *Scots Magazine*, and this work reached a peak in my chosen year, 1946. She was writing poetry and prose, often about her troubling childhood, with a number of poems also about the deaths of contemporaries in the war. The beauty of Nature was also a favourite theme, and she often quoted Wordsworth, especially 'Tintern Abbey' with its celebration of youthful 'wild ecstasies'. Her favourite modern author was Neil Gunn, whose work centres so often on 'moments of delight'. In 1945, one of her poems, 'Fir Wud', took the attention of her literary idol, Neil Gunn, and he wrote to her out of the blue: 'I have just read 'Fir Wud' in Scots Magazine. A first class poem judged by highest standards. If you would continue to write poetry of that quality you would do more for Scottish literature than by any amount of prose'. Here is that poem, which is also reprinted in *Somewhere Beyond*. Gunn was right indeed to spot the quality here, where Kesson expresses her 'immersion' in the wood in physical, sensual, sexual terms: it conveys the experience unforgettably.

Fir Wud

Happit fae daylicht's cauld clarity.
Hidden the road.
An' here for lang
A yalla-yitie quietens the warld's steer,
An' mortal thochts,
Wi' the lift o's sang.
Like velvet atween ma hot bare taes
The fir loam sifts.
Birstlin' things stick till ma claes
An' the foosty guff o' an ancient wud drifts
Ower and bye.
If, forivir in this wud I jist could lie
An' tine ma thochts,
An' smell the resin, loam-filled air,
An' watch the queer wud dirt gaither
Tae battle on ma hair!
Sharpenin' draughts nip owre ma face.
Nivir sae wide awak', I shut ma een;
Syne, like a lustful quine,
Gie a' masel' tae the wud's embrace.

Gunn had a very good relationship with J B Salmond, the Editor of the *Scots Magazine*, who reliably paid him for articles to underwrite his production of fiction. He had contributed various regular series. In 1940 and 1941 he wrote 'Memories of the Months' under his pseudonym of Dane McNeil, and in 1942 this metamorphosed into 'A Countryman's Year', January to December. He stopped the series then, when his biographers say he was at the height of his success (HL 199) and also point out that his life became overcrowded with war-related matters and post-war-planning committees. The series ceased altogether in December 1942, until January 1946, with the publication of 'Country Dweller's Year' by Ness MacDonald, with Kesson also choosing a pseudonym – her own maiden name - for the series. Kesson firmly believed that Gunn had secured her this commission, and was elated: 'I'm a *real* writer now'.

So in 1946 she continued work on the farm – or farms, because as we will see there were household removals, brought up her little girl, made successful attempts to entrench herself with the BBC in Aberdeen, creating two programmes that she wrote and performed in herself. These were 'Over the Sea to Skye', a twenty-minute memory of her happy time there before the war, broadcast in March, and 'Apples Be Ripe', subtitled 'An Aberdeenshire Autumn', dealing with the different faces of autumn in country and city, broadcast in September. This was only the beginning as regards the BBC, and she had a whole career in front of her as a writer for radio, but 1946 was primarily the year of her greatest success as writer for periodicals.

Besides the twelve articles called 'Country Dweller's Year', the *Scots Magazine* published five relatively lengthy prose pieces under her own name. One was a story in Scots, 'Ferm Deem', which is available now in *Somewhere Beyond*. The others concentrated on childhood experience, remembering churchgoing, orphanage, Abriachan and the death of the unloved Invalid Aunt who jealously fought against the child Janie in *The White Bird Passes* and 'Until Such Times'. The *Scots Magazine* also published three poems, 'Abriachan Summer', 'Dusk' and 'Autumn Dyke' (also in *Somewhere Beyond*). Kesson remarks in 'February' of 'Country Dweller's Year' that she always prefers hedges full of life to hard stone walls, but this poem gives a very characteristic picture of her response to one occasion where the 'sober' dyke is overwhelmed by nature, again joyfully expressed in part in sexual imagery. This poem also features as the beginning of the radio piece 'Apples Be Ripe'.(p. 59) Kesson enjoyed relating the origins of her title:

> Once wrote an autumn script for Scotland. I called it 'Apples Be Ripe', from a very old English folksong. Producer liked the title, asked its source. She's very sweet, very lovely, but shy and reserved. I never forgot the expression on her face when I told her the verse from which the title was taken:
>> Apples be ripe
>> And nuts be brown.
>> Petticoats up
>> And trowzers down!
> We used it nonetheless! (WHL 184)

But for all the power of these poems, prose was to be her basic medium. It is often a very lyrical prose, but moments like this are rare:

Autumn Dyke

A stretch o' sober dyke gairds a' the corn,
Like some auld-farrant chiel with-haudin' his gowd-haired quines
Frae burstin' in flamboyant ecstasy.
An' a' the while they shak' their heavy tresses
An' reeshle in their laughter secretly.
Syne, farrer on, flauntin' the dyke intae obscurity
The hips an' haws afire, gleamin' wi' rain.
That autumn nicht put blindness on tae me.
I'll niver see the lang stane dyke again.
In spring an' summer, ay, in winter, tae,
I'll see the lauchin' corn an' the reid hips
Weet wi' the rain.

The North-East Review had to fold in October 1946 for lack of funds, but before that Kesson contributed copiously, with 8 major prose pieces, often superficially fictionalised. These included 'I Must Not Dream', the tale of a little girl being punished at school for hearing and responding to poetry being taught to the older pupils at the other end of the room. 'Judgment' is a story where the orphanage children discover and consume the stale biscuits being kept for the hens, and are dealt with, far from sternly, by the 'Mannie', the Matron's husband. 'Makar in Miniature' which would also in time be adapted for radio, was the most successful attempt to date to deal with the material of Kesson's childhood, and the outline of *The White Bird Passes*.

And there were also the twelve fairly short essays which make up 'Country Dweller's Year'.

There is no internal evidence in these of upturned life and domestic crises. There is no clear evidence of where the writer is living, except that it is a poky cottar house, or whether she moves. In fact there is little evidence of any kind: it is as hard in 1946 as in any other of Kesson's cottar years to establish any details of changes of address, as she rarely dated her letters, and often omitted address as well. But from surviving evidence, largely thanks to correspondence with the BBC, it is evident that in January and February the family was living at Wester Calcots, Elgin. When the next move took place is unclear, but in October Kesson writes to Moultrie R Kelsall at the BBC from Hill of Fiddes Cottages, Udny Station, some eleven miles from Aberdeen. This is where she had her thirtieth birthday, and where she wrote to Moultrie Kelsall, sending an early attempt at a self-portrait for radio, and confiding in passing:

> I am very tired. Our house was falling about our ears – it was condemned sixteen years ago! And so we flitted to the above address. I've been working – creating mentally. I'm expecting an addition to my family - creating physically – so between flitting and a' thing else I'm fair scunnered!

They were still at Hill of Fiddes in November, and it is impossible to tell now what made them move back north to Coulardbank Cottages, Lossiemouth in December, with Kesson nine months pregnant, but it was at home in Coulardbank Cottages that Kenneth Kesson was born on the 29th of December. From Lossie she was able to resume her six-monthly visits to her mother, now badly incapacitated with syphilis, in Craigmoray Institute in Elgin. But the rigours of cottar life persisted: in April 1947 she was writing again from Lossiemouth, 'half my roof has fallen in'… The reader of 'Country Dweller's Year' knows nothing of falling roofs or pregnancy, of changes domestic or geographical: the reader is admitted into a nearer intimacy with the writer.

I want to draw attention to 'Country Dweller's Year', for two reasons: the series is unique in that it offered the writer freedom to write about her immediate, contemporary and personal experience, and secondly because here she most uninterruptedly was able to concentrate on the aspects of country life she loved passionately – although her love of trees and woods, for example is found everywhere in her work, from *The White Bird Passes* and *Where the Apple Ripens* to *Another Time, Another Place*. Her full awareness of this passion for the land came gradually: it could still take her by surprise when she was writing about *Glitter of Mica* in 1982:

> I think I have just this minute realised at least one of the reasons for writing it, a tremendous feeling for the land itself. Innate in me from my very first consciousness . . . I have always felt far more for places than I have for people. I carry climates within me. (WHL 258)

When Kesson identifies herself in 'Country Dweller's Year', she writes as a cottar wife, living in a poky cottar house. She walks to Elgin daily at one point, and mounts an ancient bike at another. She is one of those engaged on working the land, and by no means always enjoys this: in 'April' she writes:

> The tattie-park makes its demands in April. No labour is as deadly as planting tatties in a drizzle. Then I become as dull in mind as the sky abune me. I have no vision other than stretches o' lang broon dreels; no hearing except the dull thud o' tatties hittin' the soil.

But most of the subject matter of these essays concerns the writer's brief moments of respite and solitude, the full-hearted response to solitude of someone habituated to living in institutions, hard against others, deprived of any privacy, in orphanage, hostel or hospital. It is notable that very few humans are mentioned at all, and these mainly by their occupations, the orra-lad, the cattlie. Her fullest response is to the natural world, especially trees and woods: she always finds a wood nearby, and quickly makes it 'my wood'. Here is a passage from 'January' that establishes her feelings: after a January ceilidh she acknowledges a more than ordinary solitude:

> Time out of mind I have stood on a silvered hill when it was neither night nor day – but the silence between.
> I have come from the closeness and intimacy of a country ceilidh, and ceilidhs in country districts have just enough interest to absorb me. When belated 'good-nights' are said, I stand for a moment looking at the door that shuts me out from its inhabitants and its cheer; I look at the great, clear, silent world stretching before me, and I am the most solitary being in existence. Solitary only until I have walked far enough from the hospitable house to throw away its songs, its laughter, its intimacy from my mind. Then I cease being solitary and become immersed into the being of a moonlit, winter's night.
> Elation predominates. I am in possession of the whole landscape. A light looming in the distance brings discord even while it brings friendliness; for, when the hoar-frost glitters under the moon; the sky has no colour but clearness; the stars flicker palely, then the night is ethereal and has no kinship with paraffin lamps glowing in wee, scattered hooses.

Time and again here and in Kesson's other work we find her attachment to the country and to woods and trees in particular. She said to Julie Davidson in 1980, 'Woods are my territory'. [1] The passion for woods is found in all her novels. Woods seem most of all for solitude – but also perhaps the particular domain of women. In *The White Bird Passes* we have the rapturous walks of Janie and Liz to Grandmother's house, in the middle of the woods. These are the 'rare enchanting' moments when mother and child are in fullest accord:

> The wood thickened and dimmed. Great patches of wild hyacinths waved darkly blue. The sky was crowded out. Moss sprang beneath their feet, and the dust of it rose like thin smoke. The foosty guff of an ancient wood drifted over and past in great imprisoning waves. The Hangman's Tree loomed high in this dark heart of things. 'Tell me all about it again, Mam,' Janie pleaded, fearful but fascinated. (p.59)

At the end of the wood the light changes:

> Meanwhile the path through the wood widened. The sky pierced its way through the trees again; hyacinths blazed truly blue. And the light of the world outside the wood surprised the eye with momentary blindness. Primroses took on their own colour again, and vetch shouted in masses along the bank.

The force of the verbs is remarkable, and typical.

Then there is that wonderful story of Grandmother when young having a piano delivered, and instead of waiting until it is taken indoors, young Grandmother played it out under the trees. Janie and her Grandmother achieve their greatest closeness out in the wood.

At the orphanage there is the Duck's Wood, where Janie early on finds refuge and solitude, but which becomes 'black with pain' after that painful farewell to her mother when she has failed to express her love. Liza has come to the orphanage, terribly altered, to ask for Janie to be returned to help her: she is suffering from syphilis, and going blind. Janie is shocked by her mother's appearance as they sit in the wood: 'The Lane, and the dream of returning to it, disintegrated in the wrecked reflection of Liza's face . . . They had sat here in the wood, crouching over the smouldering ashes of old loyalties, trying to coax them into flame again'. (p.119) As she used in the Lane, Janie asks her mother to promise again that she won't die for a long, long time. But Janie is no longer protected by naïve innocence: here she has to try to create her own protection: 'But, knowing now that people couldn't truly make such promises, had sat quietly, filling her eyes and mind with the long lengths of the great trees and shutting out the brooding image of death'. (p.122)

In *Where the Apple Ripens* the Loch Wood regularly affords some privacy for the older girls to share their secrets and their giggles. Even Isabel's mother, the sensible Kate Emslie, escapes to Corbies' Wood in search of eggs from hens that have been laying away, and returns with 'a bright expectancy of look, searching the kitchen, as if she hoped for some transformation. Her hair, in some wild escape from the bun that usually held it tight with such severity, ruffled in curls round her forehead. She must have been pretty once! Isabel realised with small, pleased surprise'. (p.28) Not long after, Isabel thinks again about her mother:

> The young girl who became her mother ran forever through cone strewn fir woods, clothed eternally in a grey frock with blue braiding at the neck, a blue calico pinny with two pockets, and black boots that buttoned right up to her knees. She always felt very close to that young girl. As if they could have been friends together. Best friends. The way herself and Else was. Sometimes, she ran ghost-like through the fir woods of her mother's stories, singing along with her. (p.63)

Even the downtrodden Isa Riddel, the almost erased wife of Hugh Riddel in *Glitter of Mica*, experiences a rare impulse:

> Like the impulse that whiles forced her to let the cows find their own way back to the byre, when May filled Ambroggan Wood with fat clumps of wild primroses; her hands that stuffed them into a jam jar, and set them on the ledge of the porch window, had some ancient surety of touch. (p. 123)

Woods and trees play a less prominent part in Kesson's radio work, for obvious reasons, but we can find them there. In 'Sleepin' Tinker', which dates from 1947, a tinker in Heaven admits to longing for the earth again: 'Eh hoo I weary for the earth again. For the wuds – for my ain bit camp and for the berry pickin'. . . wis it a gweed season at Blairgowrie this year? Tell ye the truth I'll aye hae mair love for a mossy wud than for this braw place wi' its golden gates an' things'. And in 'Highland Spring', also from 1947, an old Highland woman remembers Spring on the Black Isle. (pp. 65-70).

The little boy Danny Kernon in Jessie's first play called *The Childhood* (1949) achieves a passionate identification with the natural surroundings at Abriachan. This clearly mirrors Kesson's own experience there, in the post-hospital year, and also incorporates some of her sore feelings about her mother when they were separated in her childhood. Danny's discovery of natural beauty gives him a new strength:

> After that I was happy, I lost need of any personal affection at all from the 'aunt'; her coldness skimmed over me, and it didn't hurt me any more. I even lost need of the near memory of my mother. I belonged so fully to my own mind, to the brave words I learned in school, to the things my eyes saw, to the music my ears heard.

Danny gradually longs no more for Glasgow and the barrows: like Kesson, perhaps, he has achieved a certain degree of invulnerability because of the direction of his love:

> My love didn't belong to the barrows any more. It belonged to things from whom I expected no affection – the things of the country, the bird and beast, yes, and the very clatter of the pails in the byre, and the smell of the byre itself. They wouldn't let me down, for they couldn't love me. I was safe with them. They would neither flatter me nor scorn me, nor turn away. They were there for ever and ever. I was safe with all these things undying. [2]

But as 'Country Dweller's Year' shows again and again, the adult Kesson knew there was no final security. In 'June', she described her two ways of walking into the town, the field-track, which she has made herself, flattening the same daisies every day, and fearing to disturb the nesting peewits: 'How thankful I shall be when the infant families of three peewits grow to maturity!' - and the wood-road: 'when time is not an important factor I take the road past the wood'. The two roads have very different qualities:

The June field of illusion, where the enchanted sunlight transforms the clover flowers from purple to crimson; buttercups from palest lemon to deep copper; grasses, from white to pale lime, to olive, to the dark, glancing green of old bottles.

'The wood-road', on the contrary,

needs infinite leisure in which to be appreciated, and, just as the field is the place of illusion, the wood, I think, is the haunt of heartbreak. The wood sent out on the mist-heavy air the sair smell that the hawthorn aye has; the hawthorn's gone to make way for the old, heavy, broom-sweet smell, and mingles it with the bitter-sweetness of the wild roses. Hawthorn – whose scent lingers after the blossoms have gone – broom, wild roses, fir trees; smell them condensed together, syne you'll understand the definition of heartbreak. . . . I never feel a trespasser on the wood-road; the birds there are so secure in their sense of possession that I am but a passing shape of no account.

Both extracts illustrate special qualities of this work – the field-track shows her fascination with colour, light and change, and her intent observation, while the 'wood-road' shows how importantly she reports on scents, and differentiates them. 'May' is the only month when she can smell the trees. And throughout she filled many lines with music and birdsong – 'Perhaps the secret of May's poignancy lies in the fact that nothing touches the human being more than smell and song.' (p. 13)

And with all this, 'Country Dweller's Year' indicates a mastery of English, combined with an occasional, well-judged use of the Doric. Also, the notes on sources of the quotations show that this farm-worker has a wide knowledge of poetry, songs she remembers from school, traditional classics like Wordsworth and Coleridge, and contemporary writers like John Drinkwater, Rose Macaulay and the Georgians.

Poems

Only three of the writer's own poems are included here, since 'Fir Wud' and 'Autumn Dyke' both appear in *Somewhere Beyond* and are reprinted in this introduction. I find both of these outstandingly successful. 'Seasons' Spell' shows an early devotion to all four seasons, similar to the themes she would embroider in 'Country Dweller's Year'. The verse, too, has similar qualities to the prose, active verbs, vivid experience of colour and scent. But the early poems I find uneven in quality, and 'Seasons' Spell' is not to my mind entirely successful, inspired by some of the Georgian poetry she was reading. It is included here to indicate her lasting interest in the topic, and the very unevenness I refer to.

'Dusk' captures a devotion to the coming of night, and celebrates in Doric the poet's experience of being 'immersed' in the now colourless country scene, 'Whaur trees, flooers, water and mase!' / Are neither alive nor dead!' 'Abriachan Summer' is an attempt to recover the aged, rooted quality of the lonely community to which Kesson was dispatched after her nightmare in the Aberdeen mental hospital: old people who have developed a serene acceptance of life, time and mortality.

Nature Prose

The journal pieces collected under this loose heading are quite varied. 'Winter's Wid' and 'Contentment', fairly unusually, are story-portraits of male characters, fearful little boy and aged but contented man, both preoccupied to some extent with the woods. The next two, 'Pilgrimage' and 'The Flowering Currant' are both typical stories spun out of Kesson's own young life, the one with memories of the Orphanage children, the other a farmworker's wife with a precious memory of a flower she found in her youth. 'May Melody' gives a glimpse of a young girl experiencing her first sexual attraction, in a context of becoming newly aware, too, of nature's May sweetness and richness, an attraction which unnerves her and makes her flee an apparently safe encounter in panic. As Kesson said once in a Woman's Hour discussion, 'A very young girl is such a mixture of spirit and animal need'.

Radio Plays

'Apples Be Ripe' is the first of Kesson's plays for radio here, and the one least recognizable as a play. It is rather a brief series of tableaux about harvest time on a farm, and has no real characters: all are typical rather than individual. Elizabeth Adair, Kesson's producer,

Kesson's first radio producer, Elizabeth Adair: their long and fruitful partnership in radio plays began in 1945. (courtesy of the late Elizabeth Adair)

might call it a feature. 'Highland Spring' on the other hand has one memorable figure, the old woman dreaming of her youth on the Black Isle. Again, though, there is no attempt to offer a plot line: it is a kind of radio Impressionism: Kesson invented new modes as she went along. Here mother and son speak in different accents, she in the Black Isle tones of her youth, and he in his Aberdeenshire Doric. It is interesting that the poems Kesson quotes here are all adapted from the Celtic feminine bard 'Fiona MacLeod', created by William Sharp. These are rarely seen now as truly Highland. I have been unable to trace the song 'Arise and follow love'.

'Over Lendrum' is longer and more elaborate. It concerns the last working day at home of Helen, a young woman desperate to leave her native village where she delivers the milk, to go to work in the city of Lendrum, which has a magical appeal for her, of romance and inchoate excitement. This piece marks a late, fine collaboration between Kesson and her first radio producer, Elizabeth Adair. It was an experiment for Adair, who pioneered experiments in Outside Broadcasting all over the North East:

> I had the idea to broadcast a rural play actually amid the stooks
> in a field (instead of in the studio, depending on mechanical
> or recorded effects) so we 'borrowed' a farm from a friend near
> Stonehaven and the cast ran across the pastures, leapt the tinkling
> burn, slapped the cows in the byre and made their exit in the
> rumbling farm-cart. This was one of Jessie Kesson's first plays
> especially written for radio and was called *Ultimate Landscape*
> [*Over Lendrum*] [3]

It was an important play for Kesson too, who was struggling to find an ending for the loosely autobiographical novel *The White Bird Passes* that would be agreeable both to herself and to her friendly but anxious publishers at Chatto and Windus. She wrote a short story, 'Ultimate Landscape', published in *The Saltire Review* in Winter 1956, and this radio feature, broadcast in October 1957, each time wrestling with very similar images, and the novel found its way into print in 1958. [4]

Broadcast Talks

The pace and tone change when we move to broadcast talks. Kesson contributed 'The Cottar's Wife' to the BBC's Farm Forum series, and there she voices her lasting criticisms – the insecurity and lack of tenure of cottar life, and the possibility of 'the sack without words', and the dreadful quality of the housing cottars were expected to be insecurely tenants of. She goes on to describe the better features of cottar life, the feelings of community, which the reader may not find adequate compensation for the rest. Kesson never ceased to voice and repeat these criticisms. There is a different tone in 'Country Years 1930-1940'. It was written for 'Woman's Hour', and so for a different audience, and here she was encouraged to sum up the years before the war, and before the cottar life, at a greater distance in time. The final piece, 'Landmarks in Time', reverts to a favourite theme, the different impact of the seasons, Autumn in particular, in the countryside and in the town.

I have made a particular effort to retain punctuation as in original unless there are obvious problems.

Isobel Murray
Aberdeen
April 2009

Johnny and Jessie Kesson caught by a street photographer (courtesy of Avril Wilbourne)

Isobel Murray interviews Kesson for student television after she received her Honorary Doctorate at Aberdeen University in April 1987 (courtesy Isobel Murray)

Country Dweller's Year

By NESS MACDONALD

January

For time, caught on the ancient wheel of change,
Spins round, and round, and round; and nothing is strange
    Or shall amaze
Mankind, in whom the heritage of all days
Stirs suddenly, as dreams half remembered do.
Whatever the year brings, he brings nothing new.
Rose Macaulay. [1]

WITH the seasonal greetings of my neighbours ringing in my ears, I turn hypocrite and give voice to a false sentiment that their *New* Year shall be happy. I have lived so close to the seasons that I know only in theory can one mark off, and define the years. In practice it is impossible. The wheat, already breering in front of my window is what definers of time would describe as the fruits of "last year's sowing." It proves that years neither begin nor end, but have continuity and utter dependence on each other.

Thus, while I feel dim regret at stripping my house of its coloured festoons, robin-decorated cards, holly, without the saving grace of berries – for I have ever loved the symbols of the Christmas festival – I feel none of the newness which many profess a new year holds for them.

As January grows older I feel reluctant admiration for my neighbouring cottar's abilities to hold on to festival without origin. Nights are spent in an atmosphere of blazing logs, tobacco-reek, slow, drawn-out tales retold without variations. I feel intense pathos when I see the work-coarsened faces of the first-horseman, the tractor-lad, the cattleman, mellow into strange, ill-fitting optimism briefly begotten of the fact . . . *it jist happens aince a year.* Their new and momentarily acquired sense of values falls oddly on my ears. . . . *Fit's a hunner pound here or there? Lord, man, it's jist naething ava.* Pathos – because well I know the horseman, tractor-lad, cattleman and myself, will probably go under the mools without glimpsing *a hunner pounds here,* and we won't need it *there!*

I watch them take their slow, apologetic leave: *ye un'erstan', missis, it's jist the New Year.*

    *   *   *   *   *   *   *

As January draws towards its close, I am glad. I recapture my sense of continuity. Where the hedge provides shelter, a pioneer snowdrop ventures up to view the immensity of a barren world. Its colossal courage might have passed unnoticed – for a very early snowdrop is as infinitesimal in appearance as it is tremendous in its quality of hardiness – only it is a childhood ploy that somehow has never gone astray in the passage of time – *to look for the first snowdrop!*

But, except for its discovery, Spring isn't even a promise. Fortunately I am blessed with the proximity of a great fir wood. Blessed, because a wood is the one place where, when time stands to get its breath, I can find the ghosts of the seasons.

Autumn has never won over the wonder of its own splendour. It long overstays its welcome, though its first fires have burned out. Bracken, in a January wood, has the colour of old, dull gold. Dead leaves forsake the precincts of their mother-trees; their common burial-ground is incongruous; they lie huddled at the feet of the fir-trees, darkly proud in the knowledge of *their* immortality. When days are glaured and rain-sodden, even immortality becomes a questionable quality. The fir-trees have no sheen; only clean, swift showers leave them glinting. The slow, thick mist-rain clings heavily over the trees. The wood becomes a drookit shadow.

This winter's wood is hedged in by shadows. The thin, interlacing bushes, unfamiliar in their nakedness, were once in wild-rose flame. But shadows are temporary things; "silvered days" startle the crawling mists [2]; and no month has clearer frosts than January; the puddled ruts of an old road lose their soft glaur; and ring hard and clear; the pools of muddy water take on the clear glint of miniature lakes and gleam through the skeletons of bramble bushes.

Sometimes the wood, the road, the whole visible world lose the dirty colour of tiredness, for,

> *Slowly, silently, now the moon*
> *Walks the night in her silver shoon.* [3]

Time out of mind I have stood on a silvered hill when it was neither night nor day – but the silence between.

I have come from the closeness and intimacy of a country ceilidh, and ceilidhs in country districts have just enough interest to absorb me. When belated "good-nights" are said, I stand for a moment looking at the door that shuts me out from its inhabitants and its cheer; I look at the great, clear, silent world stretching before me, and I am the most solitary being in existence. Solitary only until I have walked far enough from the hospitable house to throw away its songs, its laughter, its intimacy from my mind. Then I cease being solitary and become immersed into the being of a moonlit, winter's night.

Elation predominates. I am in possession of the whole landscape. A light looming in the distance brings discord even while it brings friendliness; for, when the hoar-frost glitters under the moon; the sky has no colour but clearness; the stars flicker palely, then the night is ethereal and has no kinship with paraffin lamps glowing in wee, scattered hooses.

Imagery holds kent countryside in its grip. Broom bushes, scraggit and ordinary in the light of common day, assume fantastic shapes, nor do they remain in separate clumps. They join forces by means of a fragile and exquisite bond; webs of hoar-frost, so faery and delicate that the desire to "feel" them becomes an urge. I run my fingers through their coldness; they have no substance, I have only succeeded in destroying something beautiful – beyond reconstruction.

A night wood as a homeward way has quite a different delight. Not even a coating of hard frost quite takes the soft resilience out of the fir-loam. My steps fall with muffled sounds. Silence in a wood is baffling; there is no bird-sound; not even the restlessness of disturbed slumbers. The moonlight filters its shafts through the trees dividing the wood into palely-lit alleys. I see my way too clearly to entangle myself amongst the friendly noise of the crackling twigs. Within the wood, I cannot see the wood, only when I'm out and beyond it do I perceive absolutely the dark, towering shapes tapering upwards against the moon-swept sky.

I shut my door against the incredible beauty of the night. I shut it without regret. "The year," as Rose Macaulay wrote, "brings nothing new." But how faithful and generous is its renewal of the things that are old!

February

JANUARY was brittle; March will be boisterous; but now is the time of breathless abandonment, for February has the eager carelessness of a young girl.

The river that forced its winter way to the sea, darkly, dourly determined, has thrown heaviness away; there is swift lightness in its flow, and brown murkiness in its depths.

Far up where the river has its source, the peaty loam softens and yields and breaks will – and substance – to February's command. Whispering their surprise over some new element in the air, brown loam and burn join forces and gather in volume down rocky gulleys, through immensities of wooded land until they reach the howe, transformed into the broad river that I know.

The seasons bring change to the light and colour of water, just as they bring change to the foliage of trees. A February river has the delicacy of a Botticelli painting – nothing is hard or definite – the surrounding trees that glower into the water's depths have neither the stark brown-ness of winter, the lime green-ness of spring, the overwhelming fullness of summer; they have blueness, the mist-blueness that is akin to dusk.

Seen in the fading light of day the trees have no outline, no early spring-raw branches, their very buds are thick, mist-blue clusters of dusk.

But the river has only this Botticelli quality in February, for then the sky forces the reflection of its colours down through dimness, down to a fitting background – the sheen of the brown water.

My view is profound. High on the slope of a railway bank I can see the wondrous pastel pinks and lemons shimmer on the water's ripple. The trees lose blueness as they recede in the distance to become pale purple guardians clustering round the ruins of a dim gray cathedral. Above me, like a great open vault, the sky reveals the secret of the river's colours. It is branded and rutted with deep furrows of pinkness that slope earthwards to soften lemon, then blend into the mulberry of night.

This month, which lends wonder to night, gives subtleness to day. The wood is still enveloped in the remnant colourings of autumn and winter, but there is newness in its bearing.

I can smell it. A wood has an old smell. No season can eliminate the damp, foostiness that rises from wood loam, but each can add its own slight essence. February gives a tang that has the bitter-sweetness of myrrh.

In this vast, cosmopolitan colony of trees only one tree has no place. It is the loveliest of trees, in barren winter it retains beauty of form. The wood overwhelms the delicacy of its one rowan-tree. Even in summer's height, the berries of this tree had no glint of coral redness, but drooped in dull russet bunches. The rowan-tree stands slightly cowed and insignificant, but I know – and I rejoice in the knowing – the rowan-tree keeps within its own secrecy the slim, delicate interlacing pattern of beauty.

Winter and spring link hands strangely. On one side the slight hedge-rows quiver with expectancy, on the *qui vive* for some mysterious sign to burst into blossom. On the other side the dyke stretches bleakly tumble-down, enclosing a park bare after the wintering of many ewes. I would have hedges round the parks; moss crawling in patches over the dyke gives it a doleful "kirk-yaird" look; the rucks blackened by winter add a final funereal touch.

I cannot agree with the poet who wrote: "So in a single night fair February came...." [4]

The days advance slowly to meet change. I have seen a wild rose desert its June to bloom in December, but it could not re-create summer.

The seasons blend into each other without suddenness. February, content to hold sway over the wood and river, leaves yet one stubble field to winter. One stubble field – for the wheat fields are green with the grip of spring; the grain fields to be lie darkly ploughed awaiting the tractor-lad, the drill machine, and the quick, satisfying hail of seed hurling down.

February, which was a rumour in January, leaves legacies to March. Like the father of the Prodigal Son, I saw it "coming a long way off."

It's like being involved in the secrecy of all days. I know what lies beneath the bleak park. I know the smell, colour and shape of what waits to surprise the hedges. I know something which the wood, with centuries of experience over it, must wait to discover. It has all to come without swiftness, but with subtle certainty. That's why I cannot say with the poet:

"So, in a single night, fair February came."

March

THESE are the days in which Wordsworth found "each minute sweeter than before," and in the calm, which descends between its ferocious, blustering moods, March subtly transforms from shrew into docile sweetness. [5]

The thrushes are aware of it. It is not that the hedges have burst overnight into countless masses of blossom; the hundreds of quivering shapes that swing on the hedges are thrushes!! They proclaim themselves. Thrushes may not be the sweetest of our songsters, but they can never be accused of lack of enthusiasm; their music rises in mass volume with such joyous effort.

I love to pass the tree or bush on which these choristers sing, solely to delight my vision. To watch them rise with one accord and fly from my approaching self, is to see something that has a magical quality – a tree recently weighed down with shape, quivering with music, suddenly, starkly empty and soundless.

Empty – but only by contrast. The pale, green renewed youth that emerges from the beech trees reflects the hitherto unnoticed oldness of their neighbouring evergreens. For this is surely a "new" month. The clean-ness that fills the whole atmosphere makes my old wood ancient. Down in its hollow where the tinkers have "squatted" all winter, rusted petrol cans, broken crockery, scraps of rags, and all the paraphernalia of a tinker-camp jar on my eyes for the first time. Winter's darkness had concealed the wood's "weak" spots; this clean wind-sweptness reveals them ruthlessly.

The yellow whin blooms that have so courageously coloured the winter have contrarily turned dimly brown in this month of renewal, but here and there along the by-road that loveliest of all blossoms – hawthorn – emerges star-eyed. It still withholds its greatest charm, its "unforgettable, unforgotten , thrilling sweet" smell which is only fully wafted through the rural world in late April and early May. [6]

The harrow slackens the wheat out of its winter fastness; the grain fields slope blackly, straightly furrowed. Here the secret continuance of the countryside is absolutely illustrated – the seeds of this year's harvest lie new-born in the earth and not two hundred yards away a steam mill threshes last year's corn. An ordinary man plans his life from day to day, a countryman must plan *his* life through incalculable years before he becomes

> *The husbandman who knows*
> *Deep in his heart*
> *The beauty of his power.* [7]

The March-born lambs in their young, white briskness intensify the shabby greyness of winter-weary ewes. But the mud-rutted bareness of their pasturage is deceptive; given a respite from hungry sheep, that same park in a brief week will be a vast green oasis. Grass is one of the things that is given swift birth out of the soil usually slow and contemplative.

      *   *   *   *   *   *   *

The only humans that are truly close to spring are the harrower and the early sower. All the farm-workers from grieve to orra-loon bend over the clipper in the neep-park for one hundred and thirty kye are still on their "winter" feed. When the neep-park is bereft of its labourers, the carts rumble past my door, their great loads of straw swaying precariously. "Howin' neeps," "plantin' tatties," "liftin' tatties," "hairst" – these are the well-known "rush" times in a country dweller's year. Yet there is no season in that life that can be taped off as a "slack" season. Nor do country dwellers ever give the impression of haste; they take each day and its work in the slow, dignified stride with which the earth sends them.

The stray straws from the disappearing cart blow into the crevices of the dike or huddle at the side of the bank, the windswept road winds barely white. The beauty of the landscape lies in colour contrast. There is no subtle blending of light and shade; great stretches of rough, black furrows slope to emerge into the pale green of exquisitely fragile beech trees. A sky devoid of cloud and blueness throws its crystal, cold clarity earthwards; the distant hills unsoftened by mist or shadow loom blackly. Indeed, this is a clean, windswept month – but sweet, too, when early morning oldens into the mild warmth of midday, and at night, when dusk comes, and the stars, so close to my wood, seem to hang in the trees.

April

TO me, April is the month that holds the essence of Spring. There are two places I love to visit in search of April. One is a high hill-slope nine miles west of Inverness. It is curious – up there where one is surrounded by crags, deep gulleys, and all the sterner stuff that goes to make a hill – to find Spring so profuse, and green, and gentle.

It would be hard to find one bit of brown earth on that hillside in April, for bracken, rightly called "lovely curse" by Highland folk, spreads like a vast, young, strong plantain, and all through the bracken, in countless multitudes, cluster primroses that are thick and yellow and smelling like spice.

The hill is composed of red rock, and in clear, Spring sunlight the rocks glow like fires.

It is so high up that you feel as if any moment you might topple into Loch Ness below. They say the loch is bottomless and treacherous, yet, on calm days, it is, as Coleridge writes, *a painted ocean.* [8]

Spring in the hills would confront the greatest artist with too vast a panorama. I doubt if he could ever capture it. For Spring there is more than colour; it is music and scent. The burns literally hum down the hillside, the trees have rhythm in their shaking. The smell of Spring in the hills is a blending of peaty thickness, bracken-mould, flowers' spicyness and clean, quick purge of the wind. Down in the hollows anenomes, bereft of smell, gleam in pale patches.

The second place to which I go to in search of April is a Morayshire wood. It spreads squarely solid for five miles on each side of the North Road. It is my conception of an absolute wood. Thick, dark oak trees emphasise its solidity; even in Spring they remain heavy and shaggy. You could explore this wood for a lifetime without exhausting its revelations. One moment you are in the heart of the wood; a few steps and you find yourself on the heights of a disused quarry; and, when this happens, if you have sensitivity, you know that all history lies in those great, moss-covered boulders, and shaggy, old trees, and that kings and wars are but incidents.

You recall from old tales told by your grandmother that this wood, and the incidents that surrounded it, were of far more moment to the folk of Moray than the Napoleonic Wars. You cannot visualise Waterloo; but you can see the stage-coaches rumbling through along the road in the darkness of night.

But it was April I came in search of; it lies in the cool, deep hollows of the wood. There, thicker and stronger and bluer than any garden dreams, are the wild hyacinths. They overwhelm the hollows. You know they grow there long before you reach them. Their clean-cutting smell immerses itself into you. Even when you arrive at the toll-house and the wood is left far behind, the hyacinth's smell sticks in your nostrils.

I have shop-bought hyacinths in a bowl, pink and white, with no sheen over them. If I were confined to live indoors forever, the hyacinths in the bowl could not bring Spring to me – not after knowing thick, wet, wild ones whose blueness glistens.

I never see those wood hyacinths without remembering: -

> *Shade-loving hyacinth, thou comest again*
> *And thy rich odour seems to swell the flow*
> *Of the lark's song, the red-breast's lonely strain,*
> *The stream's tune heard best sung where wild flowers grow*
> *And ever sweeter where the sweetest blow.* [9]

The tattie-park makes its demands in April. No labour is as deadly as planting tatties in a drizzle. Then I become as dull in mind as the sky abune me. I have no vision other than stretches o' lang broon dreels; no hearing except the dull thud o' tarries hittin' the soil.

But when the days are mild, I become benevolent. I can "jook" when the toon bairns – in the exuberance of their brief country freedom – forget that the tatties are for planting, and aim them at random. I even forget to be angry when a tattie hits the target.

And I can absorb those strange "out-laws" – the tinker bairns, congregated together, working nimbly, cursing each other enthusiastically, and every now and again forgetting to watch out for "the grieve", forgetting to plant tatties, forgetting everything except the fact that they are tinkers, and, as such, the natural enemies of other bairns. An age old battle begins; the weapons used are tatties. "The grieve" calls a truce.

"Damn ye a'! Can ye nae wark yer wark without mischief? If ye'd pit the tatties in o' the dreel as fast's ye're slingin' them at each ither, the hale park wad be planted."

The old inborn fear of "superiors" quells the battle in the tinkers' zone. There is hard work – and hard silence – for about ten minutes; syne I smile with real joy, when a wee tinker loon sings shrilly, nonchalantly

Good-bye to the Red River Valley [10]

But as I said, for the April that comes of its own accord I go to the hills – or woods.

O dreamy, gloomy, friendly trees
  I came along your narrow track
To bring my gifts unto your knees,
  And gifts did you give back,
Ye vastest breathers of the air
  Shook down with slow and mighty poise
Your coolness on the human care,
  Your wonder on its toys,
Your greenness on the heart's despair,
  Your darkness on its noise. [11]

May

MANY poets have felt the spirit of their art move them in May. The verse, which conjures May for me, was written by a poet whose name I have forgotten. I knew his verse in childhood.

> *Ah, 'tis like a tale of olden time long, long ago,*
> *When the world was in its golden prime*
> *And Love was lord below.*
> *Every vein of earth was dancing with Spring's new wine,*
> *'Twas the pleasant time of flowers*
> *When I met you, love of mine.*[12]

In these lines I still find the poignancy of May.

"The pleasant time of flowers" – but it is neither in the glow of lilies – the white ones which belong to early summer – nor in the clusters of dusty millers shedding their crimson along the borders, nor in the trailing purple of "cats' mint" that I find the May of the verse, but in the byways and woods.

May is the month which is more mature than Spring, less mature than Summer; it is almost in itself. I can smell May more sensitively than I can see it. There is a "nip" over all the briar hedges. If I but shut my eyes, the wild roses, which are only curled buds, instantly flame the hedges. Their sweet, sharp scent precedes their blossoming time, that scent more intense now than it will be when the roses themselves appear in June.

So with the trees; in no other month will I be able to smell the trees; their sticky, heavy sweetness will have outgrown its strength with the increase of foliage.

The hawthorn, whose smell has engulfed early May, dies at May's end with the same exquisite loveliness with which it lived; slim white corpses flutter earthwards till the narrow byway becomes as white as any winter.

May *is* poignant. The birds' song is at its sweetest now. Daylong its volume rises from the wood as though the singers' hearts would burst with the fullness of their tune. Perhaps the secret of May's poignancy lies in the fact that nothing touches the human being more than smell and song. May is the month of both.

                    *   *   *   *   *   *   *

The vivid green of the corn parks contrasts strangely with the insipid whitish-green of the neighbouring hay-fields. All the farm labour is concentrated in the neep park. A curious scene to witness. One tractor-lad sows the manure, another tractor follows in his wake to open the drills – and lastly a solitary horse walks slowly into its undisputed own, pulling the turnip-sower. In front of this mechanised busyness the manual labourers, who can never quite be replaced, clear the park of weeds. For, like all things that are produced from the soil, there's a lot mair tae neeps than jist the atein' o' them!

Now my wood begins to lose its secrecy; a secrecy that will only drift through it again when October's brambles become too crined and shrivelled for folk to pick. The raid on the wood is neither sudden nor mass. Gradually the courting couples filter into it with the lengthening nights. Sunday afternoons bring an influx. Even on week-days the wood begins to lose its solitude. Those for whom courting days are but a memory come to it in urgent search for fire-wood.

The breaking of dried sticks is a friendly sound, and I love the sicht of an auld wife wi' a shawl roon' her heid and a burden o' sticks on her back.

Later on, when the rhododendrons are in bloom, the bairns from the toon's "closes" will forsake their own environment and swoop down on the wood. I've yet to see any more delightful aspect of laughter than the sight of a small urchin wi' nae bottom till his breeks hugging a great armful of rhododendrons with a nonchalance that is only destroyed by his shouts to a wee lass in front of him: "Hey, you! Fan we come tae the toon ye've tae bide ahint an' cairry this flooers. If ye dinna 'a'll burst ye!"

                    *   *   *   *   *   *   *

With the coming of the Essential Works Order May has lost some of its significance for the farm-worker. [13] No longer does "the term" fill the roads with long processions of "flittin's". And no longer is the conversation in cottar kitchens full of doubts and hopes about "the new place and the new maister." But May is ever May, sweet to look at, sweet to smell, sweet to hear.

June

I AM not a naturalist. I only know that each day I take a near cut through the fields to the town. My near cut has taken on the aspect of a beaten track. The track owes its origin to sentiment. I made it for myself. Daisies, which lose their whiteness when the sun shines fully on the field to take on the sheen of silver, are so profuse that each step of mine cuts down the lives of these rightful owners. Hence my track. By destroying a few I preserve the multitude. When the sun has gone, I return to find the field curiously empty, the daisies have gathered their immensities of whiteness into curled, rose balls.

The daily sojourns through this field fill me with a real sense of guilt. Perhaps from a bird's high vision I do have the appearance of a terrorist. How thankful I shall be when the infant families of three peewits grow to maturity! Two frenzied feathered mothers wheel and mourn, and resort to subterfuge against the nameless terror of my approaching self, somewhere in proximity to their young.

The field is immense; no one, and least of all, the peewits, can hear or understand my assurance: *Haud yer skirlin' tongues! I dinna even ken faur yer nests are.*

The third mother, unlike her companions in suspense, is stoical. She doesn't attempt to lead me on a false trail. She sits on the top of the telegraph pole awaiting destiny, giving voice to her fears in shrill, drawn-out cries.

When time is not an important factor I take the road past the wood. The field-track, the wood-road. How strangely the two roadways are contrasted! The field holds all illusions in its clover-shadowed grass. I have outgrown daisy-chaining; but I think about it. There is sweetness to be got out of the sucking of clover flowers and red sorrel; I have outgrown that, too; but I remember it. There is legend where the field slopes up to become a railway bank in the form of white "thunder-flowers" – which somehow never induced thunder at the request of childlike gods.

"Sticky Willies" are still practical jokers, entwining themselves round my legs, but I'm too old to be amused.

The June field of illusion, where the enchanted sunlight transforms the clover flowers from purple to crimson; buttercups from palest lemon to deep copper; grasses, from white to pale lime, to olive, to the dark, glancing green of old bottles.

When the sun gives place to the trickery of shadow, the field loses smoothness; long lines of hills rise up where the shadows lay their lengths. Now is the buttercups' hour; the small white and blue flowers, content with holding the day, sink down into imagined hollows; the field is held in shadow, with only the bronze of night buttercups to give it colour.

And, in all this immense stretch of immense illusions, the real flower of illusion has no place; it flaunts a field away – tremulous redness, but I never trespass over the domain of the green-lacquered corn, the red-lacquered poppies.

The wood-road needs infinite leisure in which to be appreciated, and, just as the field is the place of illusion, the wood, I think, is the haunt of heartbreak. The wood sent out on the mist-heavy air the sair smell that the hawthorn aye has; the hawthorn's gone to make way for the old, heavy broom-sweet smell, and mingles it with the bitter-sweetness of the wild roses. Hawthorn – whose scent lingers after the blossoms have gone – broom, wild roses, fir trees; smell them condensed together, syne you'll understand the definition of heartbreak.

Still, my wood-road has comfort, too, begotten from the very depth and coolness and shelter and stability of a wood.

The soreness it sends out has no kinship with "natural sorrow, loss, or pain" [14]; it is just as the poet says, "feeling the heartbreak in the heart of things." [15]

The morning wood-road is a way of scents. The evening wood-road is a coloured canvas with its background of tremendous green. Then the pink and while petals of the roses diminish to reveal their red-gold hearts; their beauty, being in their delicacy, makes the neighbouring polished rhododendrons acquire vulgarity; the broom bushes skirt the wood, stretches of small fires; the speedwells, vetch, violets lose tangible shape, and are but tiny blue shadows flitting in the grass.

I never feel a trespasser on the wood-road; the birds there are so secure in their sense of possession that I am but a passing shape of no account.

But is there security? A pigeon, white and still lovely to the touch, lay on the pathway, as beautiful as life itself, except for the shot-mark. I do not know the laws governing the preservation of wild life. I know that, even in death, this pigeon looked out of place lying on the naked roadway. I put its body where it belonged, inside the wood. The incident took all the beauty out of the evening.

July

The longest day has come and gone; yet there is about July a sense of infinite abiding. It is as though summer, having now reached its zenith, is reluctant to be deprived of its glory.

The wood has lost its subtle charm of light and shade. It has but one colour – a green that stretches endlessly and tires the vision. The whole landscape is heavy and flamboyant.

Man, they say, ought always to look upwards; the exception to that rule is when the place is a wood and the month is July. This is the place and time when you find it a relief to take your eyes away from the still, thick, dusty foliage overhead, and cast them downwards to the soothing aspect of cool, dark loam. You are grateful for the delicacy of remaining clusters of *Stars of Bethlehem*, white and beloved, because July is a month curiously bereft of delicacy. It is simply a maturer version of June, and, unlike the other months of the calendar, July has but slight essence of its own.

Slow to fruit, the late-flowering bramble-bushes straggle dirtily white, enabling the byway to maintain its semblance of white hedgerows.

The drought that has persisted through the summer has covered every leaf, flower and blade of grass with a complete coating of grey dust.

Escape from dust, heat, and oppressive weight is only to be found by the river's banks, deep in the wood, or, if the refugee is as fortunate as I, up where "swift-rinnin' Spey" tumbles through the hills.

There the wind never quite falls, and the world is always cool. The tree-covered slopes retain the fresh greenness of spring. Perhaps distance is responsible for this illusion; or it may be that high up on Speyside the seasons are slower. I've seen yellow primroses bloom in the gardens at Aberlour in late June.

And so in July the distant hills glow faintly blue through the branches of slender, white-blossomed rowan trees. Beeches are still palely green and brittle; the very remoteness of hill-scenes gives them ethereal coolness.

The great face of rock by the bridge that takes us into the outskirts of Aberlour glows like a jewelled wall, red like rubies, and clear under the trickery of the sun – like diamonds. It is a flowered wall, too. Slight green ferns have found a swaying footing on its face; bluebells cluster on its ledges; small yellow flowers like miniature whins shoot out from its crannies. Far below, a deep brown foreground, rumbles the Spey.

July, bringing no new flower, brings no new fragrance. What slight essence it has is to be smelt along the edge of the garden where the black and red currant bushes throw out their own musky scents.

Nor does the hayfield diffuse its wonted sweetness. Drought is the enemy of essence, and the countryside has its times for everything. Its fragrance is in the dew-heavy mornings and wet-mist nights.

When summer was in its first clarity and freshness, I was glad to leave the damp pokiness of my house behind. But now that summer stands still to brood, I am thankful for my cool, stone floor, my bare white walls, my kitchen window, so small that it limits my vision and admits only a slight expanse of overgrown hedge. Overgrown is a mild adjective; the hedge is as tall and thick as a copse. In spring a kindly neighbour offered to trim my hedge. I have a horror of a "trained" garden. I like unlimited greenery around me, and my refusal to have the hedge trimmed solved the housing problem for a multitude of thrushes who day-long sing their gratitude.

August

Why should we sorrow that Summer's dazzling ray
So soon has passed away,
Whilst we can borrow from Autumn's mellow light
A scene more truly bright?[16]

THAT old song was not written to convince me of Autumn's superiority as a season. I have always felt the charm of the months that go to make up "the fall". But August has little of the atmosphere of decline about it. It has something of the briskness, of the newness of a Spring month. July's lethargy has gone to be replaced by days spacious and clear; days in which there is room enough to breathe.

On the farm this *is* "breathing time". The farm-workers who are not on their brief annual summer holiday – of three days' duration – scythe the thistles round the steading and fill the day with odd jobs. The pace of their life has slowed down. It is as if the men and the earth they work were conserving the last ounce of strength for "the hairst."

Thistles are scythed down silently and so there is an odd stillness all over the airt of the usually industrious farm. But sounds of labour issue from the wood and from all along the burnside, where the wild rasps grow so profusely. The labour is a labour of love judging by the shouting of the bairns who have escaped from the town to "pu' rasps."

Autumn, like all seasons, rings its changes gradually, but August in itself is less conservative. The few wild roses which remain are flaunted into obscurity by the vividness of the red hips sharing their bushes. Colour has reached its most flamboyant peak. The tattie-park has its own display of flowers. Seen in the slanting angles of the sunlight the flowers range in colour from palest heliotrope to deep mauve, and from primrose yellow to orange. In the wood beech-nuts are still green in colour but heavy in crop. At the month's end all greenery disappears from the grain parks, the corn is solidly, harshly brassy in colour and its stalks in texture are almost as brittle as the straw they will ultimately become.

What trace of Autumn August brings is to be found in the

wood. There in the wood's depths the sun has forgot his burning fire, the light is subdued, the pine needles dimly russet lie scattered on the dusty moss. The beeches and oak-trees are still heavily green – but it is the last lap of their greenness. The birds' exquisite Spring songs are over; their mature, full-throated Summer songs are silent, but the blackbird shrieks, the wood-pigeon flaps his wings, grasses rustle, insects hum their swan-song, twigs creak; song has given place to sound.

There is a subtle trace of Autumn in the August nights. Dusks begin to return again. Warm, mellow day has belonged to Summer, but the filtering, violet-blueness of night is infused with that "burnt fires" smell peculiar to Autumn.

Through the night's stillness the sounds of carnival drift from the town like some alien quantity. The peewees' shrill, sorrowful "weep" is just part of an Autumn night, and as such becomes part of country folk's environment. But music from the chair-o'-planes is unusual and exciting. The young folk cycle carnival-wards with insistent haste, for with the approach of the short days carnival will soon disappear. To Carnival then while it lasts and we are young! And to the old and middle-aged the peewee's cry, an August night, and the approach of Autumn.

September

Earth seems to squander
Her plenty on the sheaf
Her gold on every leaf. [17]

THE rains have, here in Morayshire, at least, flattened much of the crop, but, for all that, extra "hairst hands" begin to filter into the farming communities; Irish labourers, who speak richly and laugh often; a newly-married townsman eager "to try" the life of the country after the heart-breaking, expensive experience of six months spent in a city's furnished rooms; the farm labourers' wives, pitching their sheaf-filled forks with the knack of long experience, but with their minds far up the parks within their small, dark cottar-houses, and their best thoughts concerned with their supper-to-be and a night's rest; the youngest orra-loon whistling day-long because it's his first hairst; it's a novelty, and he hasna yet haen time tae tire. That's "hairst" – and some of the folk who make "hairst"! They hurry slowly; they're born with the instinct that hairst is the climax of their labours, that it is an insistent fundamental thing like eating, and sleeping and living; - they share this knowledge with the poet who wrote:

I hear the rickyard fill
With gossip as in generations gone,
While wagon follows wagon from the hill.
I think how, when our seasons all are sealed,
Shall come the unchanging harvest
From the field. [18]

The end of hairst brings the secretly-liked "lang nichts." Summer had its own charms, but it's in the autumn nights that the country-wife can "settle doon" in the lamp-light. It's now that the countryside begins *tae growe sma'er, mair compact and mair intimate.* Cut off from external diversions by the vagaries of the weather, the short days, the country-folk metaphorically sit back and find satisfaction and warmth in the comforting thought: *we're a' here thegither.*

The last bramble-pickers haunt the precincts of the wood; they seem like shadows rather than like people, as they bend over the ditch; their exuberance is gone. They leave the wood – and many unpicked brambles – while it is still early evening. On the road townwards their animation returns; they talk and laugh; they are no longer shadows, they are people, happy, because they are homeward bound; in half an hour they will be back in the town, in known territory, away from the strangeness of a vast wood, unfamiliar to them at all times, but overwhelming in the gloaming of a September night.

It is the wood that heralds September – suddenly, flamboyantly. It seems as though it was just yesterday that I looked across and saw the wood still in its summer green – and the next day I looked across to see it smouldering red and yellow – like some vast furnace against a dark background. For the wud is mainly a fir-wud; its beeches and oaks make its autumn.

Even the prosaic railway-bank has caught its share of September's colour. St John's Wort, vividly yellow, has the persevering quality of some everlasting flower; in relays it brightened the summer, and it lags into September profuse in quantity, delicate and lovely in structure. Crimson foxgloves blaze along the dyke-side, bluebells bloom nonchalantly out of their season; clusters of dark moss sober the flaunting scene.

In October, autumn becomes sombre, but now in September, there is no quality of sadness. For clear, sun-lit brightness this month surpasses summer itself; it may be the vast, gold background of grain-parks that gives this impression of boundless clarity and brightness; it's carried heavenwards, the sky is so white and windswept.

When I go to the town in September the contrast between autumn in town and country is overwhelming. When it's rush hour I stand in a daze, jostled and buffeted by a hurrying mass. I find some quality of terror in vast crowds of people, all of them unknown; all of them in a hurry; there is something ruthless in their haste. It's so different in the country; we all know each other, and we hurry slowly. Every aspect of the landscape is familiar to us, and autumn has touched it all; but in the town you never know that autumn's come, there's nothing to herald it. I'm aye glad when I've mounted my auld bike and have bidden the town a tearless farewell. Then rattling through the countryside in the autumn dusk I'm myself again – and happy:

The last light upon the wolds is done,
And silence falls on flocks and fields and men,
And black upon the night I watch my hill
And the stars shine – and all is still. [19]

October

THE strange charm of October is something that has come up the years with me. October was birthday month and it held Hallowe'en. Now, of course, I'm too old to have a birthday, but I can still find witchery in the gloom of any October night.

Day itself is furnace-coloured. Trees have the brooding aspect of doomed things. It is uncanny – almost as if they sensed instinctively that their resilience has left them till a distant spring. Sometimes, when the wind sweeps through the wood, "false" resilience returns to the beech trees. Their remaining leaves rustle dryly and sway stiffly before making their first – and last – contact with the loam that reared them. The sensitive onlooker has the curious feeling that he is watching a graceful, poignant moment in a ballet scene.

But day passes, and with its passing this elusive grace disappears from the wood. October nights are stark, intense, and every night is a Hallowe'en. Darkness is heralded by grotesquely-shaped shadows; the wind sombre in sound, reckless in attack, cackles at its own devilry; the leaves go to earth almost soundlessly;

> *The dusk is full of sounds, that all along*
> *The muttering boughs repeat.*
> *So far, so faint, we lift our heads in doubt;*
> *Wind, or the blood that beats within our ears,*
> *Has feigned a dubious and delusive note*
> *Such as a dreamer hears.* [20]

That is the wood. And, although we live in the "ilka day" familiarity of our cottages, the wood is the background of our lives. We welcomed its spring, rejoiced in its summer, replenished our fires in its autumn; and now, though we become remoter from it in person, it still figures largely in our minds and in our conversations. The glow from our firesides transforms our conceptions of the wood.

It becomes the legends we tell on a winter's night. It is the breeding-place of all our remembered ghosts and recollected adventures. It even becomes the threat that settles our disgruntled bairns: "If ye dinna gang till yer beds this very meenit, ye'll gang oot tae the wud for the nicht!" For, apart from unknown terrors like ghosts, the wood has become the winter abode of those "eternal squatters" – the tinkers. For the next few months the wood is something that we glance at furtively in the passing, or view from the security of our scullery window, but with which we have no intimacy after dusk; not when the tinkers' voices rise from its depths in drunken song and drunken anger. Civilisation – in the form of ourselves – is aye embarrassed at contact with the primitive.

The farm labourers' brief respite, after the ardours o' leadin' the hairst, is over; the "tattie hairst" is near. The end of this month catches the lilt of an old song in the voices of the bairns forming the tattie squads:

> Fa saw the tattie-lifters,
> Fa saw them gaun awa'?
> Fa saw the tattie-lifters
> Mairchin' doon bi Balahaugh?
> Some hiv sheen an' some hiv stockin's,
> Some hiv nane ava.
> So fa saw the tattie-lifters
> Mairchin' doon bi Balahaugh? [21]

The song was maybe appropriate twenty years ago. The young tattie-lifters who sing it now sing wi' their tongues in their cheeks. They've a' got baith "sheen an' stockin's," and they earn as much in one day as the bairns who first sang the song earned in a week. "Tattie-holidays" and tattie-lifting has become an institution like queueing; it is more an adventure now than dire need to earn a supplementary copper – and it never was a task for those whose bones hinna haen time tae "set" yet. They supply cheer and laughter for their adult fellow-workers, and anxiety for the "grieve," who, according to his nature, either shouts loudly or wheedles so that the bairns "lift their stages betimes."

This is the last insistent task on the farm before winter settles itself firmly in its groove. The last "stage" o' tatties lifted, and syne the hale landscape sinks intae placidity – the queer, uncertain placidity o' an October nicht.

November

"IF winter comes . . . . . . " Winter *has* come. And somehow I feel that spring *is* far behind in those dark, drawn-out November days.[22] I feel a sense of timelessness in a world shadowed with fog. The erstwhile intimate countryside has become remote; the known wood but a shape looming in the mist. Its tinker occupants merge silently among its shadows, for only at night does the soft-footed tinker acquire reality. Then it may be snatches of drunken song that drift from the wood, or fervent curses that echo upwards – but always intermingling with the sounds of sane living; a bairn greetin'; an antrin tinker playin' a chanter.

The old order has changed. Short years ago November was one of the two months marked apart in the farm workers' year. It held joyous Martinmas. Then did the farm servant receive his six months' "fee." His pockets jingled; his wife wore a new floral "peenie;" his loons war "rigged" wi' new beets. And, happy in the knowledge that any outstanding accounts wi' the "soutar" or the grocer were honourably closed, he himself asked little more than a jaunt to the nearest town, a meeting, a crack, and a pint with those of his kind; the relaxing, exquisite knowledge of a whole day's respite from labour. And yet, contrarily enough, the bar of the "Gordon Arms" hummed wi' a braid Scots conversation that embraced naething outside the limits o' "the Mains," "the maister," *and* "the wark" – subtle busman's holiday!

Now the farm servant's status has been modernised. He's the proud possessor of a "forty-eight hour week." All gains bring their own losses. Martinmas and all its local colour and joyousness has disappeared from the farm servants' calendar.

The greyness that characterises November's day loses its indefiniteness when night comes. The mists dispel to give place to clean, thin darkness. The wood is no longer a vague shape; it is a stark outline; the sheep on the one remaining park of pasture drift soundlessly.

> . . . . . *Than these November skies*
> *Is no sky lovelier. The clouds are deep;*
> *Into their grey the subtle spies*
> *Of colour creep.*

The huge, great clouds move gently;
Holding in bright caprice their rain.
And when of colours none,
Nor rose, nor amber, nor the scarce late green
Is truly seen. . . . . [23]

It is only the poets who can see beauty in the November night skies. Town folk never see them, and country folk have too often watched the fragile beauty of spring, the full loveliness of summer, the striking flamboyance of autumn to trouble about the obscure beauty of November. The first month of winter is inscrutable; plain folk don't understand it. In it there is neither sowing, growing, nor reaping – just long waiting.

Still those days of waiting are spent in an atmosphere of labour that is not confined to any special season. Any time and every time is ploughing time. The constant whirr of threshing mills hums through the November countryside. On mist clear days the sight of a threshing mill piled high with barley sheaves brings summer back to mind and autumn is a tang in the air.

The fields stretching vastly and barrenly make the landscape seem unlimited, but in the park beside my cottage the orramen bend ower the neeps; their spasmodic whistling cuts through the solitude; whiles they forget "the clipper" and straighten their backs to converse for a moment. They speak of the hairst that is over, they speak of Hogmanay that is to come, but November, grey and vast above them, passes unmentioned.

December

THIS is a time when I find it difficult to look at the countryside impersonally. I see it as it were, with "Christmas eyes." I can now pass the great fir wood unseeingly, but the glow and glint of the most obscure holly tree catches my eye. I sniff the air expectantly. The sentimentalist in me keeps hoping for a white Christmas. And even when my expectations are not fulfilled, when my eyes keep beholding a black, ploughed world, I can still console myself that night will come – night which is never really dark even without the aid of moonlight, for December nights, one and all, have a silver glint and a promise of white frost in their smell.

It may be my "Christmas vision" that aye makes December stars lose their distance and come so near to earth that they seem to be twinkling in the region of my kitchen-lum itself.

And it is strange, too, that I, an ordinary cottar wife, should always during this month lose touch with my own commonplace environment, my daily round, my common task, and become almost "fey," seeing in every bright star the tale

> . . . . . *my childhood used to know,*
> *I would follow it through the gloom,*
> *Hoping it might be so.* . . . [24]

But, fortunately perhaps, the whole countryside doesn't share my "feyness". "Inchbroom," the neighbouring farm, had *their* wheat sown in November and now our tractor-lad is harrowing what will be our wheat parks, his whistling cuts shrilly above the hum of his tractor.

I know that it isn't the thought of Christmas that makes *him* whistle. In the brief minutes of mutual companionship when all the farm-hands collect together in the stable to wait for "the grieve and orders," the main topic of conversation will be Hogmanay and the scarcity of whisky, and an argument is to begin – and to continue throughout the whole of this month *and* next – between the two remaining horsemen as to which of them "will keep toon" (i.e., feed and groom the horses) on New Year's Day.

Christmas remains unmentioned; it is something that has significance for the married farm workers solely because they've got bairns. And bairns have a habit of being insistent about Christmas.

Only the cattleman remains aloof from those seasonal discussions. The nature of his work means that he works alone – and none share his thoughts.

He is a queer chiel; whiles I wonder if "the cattlie" *does* share my temporary feyness. He is tall, sombrely built, more like an undertaker than a farm servant – and his eyes contradict all impressions of him, they are always full of laughter. His farm colleagues dismiss him casually as being "far frae richt."

And yet "the cattlie" is a craftsman. The new status and amenities eagerly accepted and taken advantage of by most farm workers are ignored by this kenspeckle figure. He has no limit to his working hours. His work is his life; and so any night, at any hour, a storm-lantern flickers from the direction of the byres. The impersonal onlooker, who catches the glow, shrugs his shoulders and concludes that "Wester Cloves cattleman's daft richt eneuch tae be workin' awa' at a' hoors." The thoughtful observer knows that either some sick beast's being attended to or a calf has been born, and that, in either event, the "daft" cattlie will forget to claim overtime.

Surely because "the cattlie" has spent the greatest part of his life among mangers he must feel the charm and truth of those December nights. I like to think so.

Or . . . maybe after a lapse of two thousand years dates become confused and no one knows the actual night of the nativity, which means that the frozen clearness of the stars has no significance; that "the cattlie" is really a simple-minded craitur who thinks of the mangers as merely places for beddin' the kye . . . I don't know. But I do know that the smell of snow hangs in the air, that reek is rising from the fresh dung in the fold, that the tractor-lad keeps whistling doggedly

> I'm nae awa' tae bide awa',
> I'm nae awa' tae leave ye. [25]

Poems

Seasons' Spell

When Dresden Spring flits by, and in her wake,
Speedwell's ethereal blue, lilies' pale gold, shy aconites,
And all her sweet, indefinite days . . .
Ripe Summer's left for me, - and vague regret,
    O not the scent drenched lilac,
    Is Spring's first violet!

But Summer casts her witching spell,
And buys me with laburnum's liberal gold,
Squandering wealth,
Within hand's reach; and over the brown road,
And brilliant vetch, shouting in masses,
A blue-banked world!
Mysterious foxgloves, in an old wood, brown with trees,
And somebody's roses, mass'd high, pink and white,
O wealth of fragrance; anybody's thorns,
Aristocratic lupins, by the river,
A panorama, winding ever,
Reluctant Summer passes o'er.
Cold Autumn's left for me, - and vague regret,
    O, not the red of rowans, hips and haws,
    Is Summer's mignonette!

But, smouldering Autumn beckons, and I go
To view a world on fire,
Reflected in the glow of tree's last braveries,
Kingly gold, triumphant red,
And hills' vermillion peaks;
The fluttering wings of laggard emigrants
And all the incense of a dying world;
Deep broom, and heather, October's last chrysanthemums,
    moor fires,
Curling to Heaven in blue, wood smoke,
White winter's left for me, - and vague regret –
    O not the first snow's fall,
    Is Autumn's swan-song yet!

And Winter holds me with a berried tree,
A snow capped church, remembered innocence,
A Tale of Mystery . . .
        O vague regret!
I think that even at the gate of heaven or hell;
Earth's lovely days will hold me fast,
And I'll remember each day's spell.

Dusk

Creep on; hap siccar wi' your velvet faulds the wearied day.
I ken nae noo familiar form o' trees.
The loch lies phantom-like alow yer mists.
Nae glitter's there, nae lithe, green limb o' earth leaps tae meet
     the wash o' wave.
Dusk owre the loch, and dusk owre a' my mind;
Like some witch o' some half-forgotten tale descendin' wi'
     slow magic fae the sky
Tae cast her spell owre ordinary earth, and owre a mortal
     watchin' by a loch.
The shape and colour a' hae fled.
I stand in a strange shrouded land,
Whaur trees, flooers, water and masel'
Are neither alive nor dead!

Abriachan Summer

Summer drifts there slow
But has its dwelling long.
It filters through the women's gossip,
Sheds its glow over the men's philosophies,
And time is not ticked off in seconds.
A summer day is all too brief
To hold Ian Dubh's reminiscences.
Nothing is lost to those among the hills;
They've seen the gulleys brown in spate
These sixty springs;
But still they pause to contemplate
Common-place things;
Calum Mor's ewe silhouetted on the crag,
The white wake of "St Ula" on the Ness,
The flails, dust grey, in Domhnull's barn
Whose usefulness they resurrect
With tales of harvests long since threshed.
They never say "The day is fine,"
But tell you why;
And that the wind will change tomorrow,
And how, in four days' time, a storm will come.
They are a race lost and involved
In all the years,
But wise, who know tomorrow is not theirs

        *   *   *   *   *

Yesterday we savoured to the full;
And, while we scythe the hay today,
We'll talk of vivid summers
Sixty years away.

Stories

Winter's Wid

Sleep jist wadna come till him. The wind ootside started frae a wee greet an' rose till a big wail, - an' dreesome the wid.

Dod could lie curled up there an' sleep, bit then Dod wis a year younger nor him, jist a bairn, and didna ken aboot the wid.

He cooried intae Dod. It hid been cauld sittin' ben the hoose; there wis a gweed eneuch fire on, bit he'd seen little o't, only a wee lowe atween the wa' an' Sandy Thomson's chair, still, he'd been lucky tae be latten bide up at a'.

Ilka time his mither cam' tae the end o' a row, she'd stick her wyvin' wire in o' her hair an' glower at him owre her specs; "Isn't it nae high time ye thocht o' gaun tae yer bed?"

Silence was golden sometimes, and he neither coaxed nor girned, he'd jist gaen himsel' a twist farther roon the back o' Sandy's chair, an' didna breathe till his mither started anither raw.

An' Sandy tellin' stories o' the wid; the wid Sandy kent, bit nae the wid *he* kent.

The wid wis the first thing he saw fin he raise, an' the last thing he saw afore he lay doon.

Green, an' bird load of simmer mornin's; promisin' a hantle o' ploys. Shadowy an' plaintive o' simmer nichts. And in the winter, baith nicht an' mornin', jist a black shape that *he* kent wis the wid.

Bit it wisna only himsel' that hid been a robber in the wid, an' it wisna only himsel' that hid focht an' drawn blood in the wid.

For Sandy wis auld, aulder nor his gran'faither, so auld that he couldna' think fit wye Sandy wisna deid.

An' Sandy kent the wid a lot langer nor he kent it . . . . "I wis comin' hame ae Friday nicht frae the market, at the back o' the year; it wis a bricht meenlicht nicht, an' I cut through the wid tae win hame suner. Jist as I cam' tae Newton Quarry I saw a mannie wi' a lang, black coat, an' big tile hat, busy diggin' a grave. I passed him by, an' nane o's passed a word. I felt gie creepy, for I kent he wis a doctor mannie lookin' for somebody tae experiment on, bit me bein' owre fifty than, an' nae haein' ony oot o' the wye trouble on me, I kent I wadna be o' muckle interest tae doctor chielies."

He wad like tae ha'e heard mair aboot the mannie in the lum hat, bit his mither speired this, an' speired that, till Sandy got fair raised an' said, "Lord, wumman, wull ye nivir believe onything yer ain een disna see?"

Syne his gran'faither tell't of hoo fan he wis a young loon, comin' through the wid ae nicht, a man jumped oot ahin' a tree, an' speired the time frae him, fin he took oot his watch, the man hit him owre the heid, an' fan he cam' till himsel' the watch hid gone.

They tell't stories o' the blue lichts that twinkled in the wid fan onybody in the Crook wis tae dee. They told o' the "Hangman's tree" an' the man that wadna hang.

A cold, fearful pleasure creepit owre him as the twa auld mannies tell't bygone tales o' the wid, wi' its robbers, an' blue lichts, an' only the sicht o' his mither wyvin' awa', wi' a queer wee lauch at the corners o' her mou' keepit him frae getting' intil a panic.

Fin Sandy rose tae go awa' hame, his gran'faither went tae the end o' the road wi' him, he creepit roon fae his chair:

"Mither, I'm feart tae gaung through tae ma bed in the dark, wi' the wid jist ootside the window, can I get a can'le the nicht?"

His mither got richt wild wi' him at first: "Gweed be here bairn! Fit wye did ye nae ging tae yer bed lang syne? Sittin' there a' nicht listenin' tae auld mannie's tales. Deil a can'le are ye getting' here!"

Syne, fin he creepit through til his bed, though she didna gie him a can'le she cam' through ahin him an' steed, lookin' through the window, oot at the wid in the darkness . Then she tell't him.

"There's naethin' tae be feart at in the wid; it's a blithe place for a bairn. There's the burn tae fish in, the rodden-trees tae mak' whistles o', trees tae climb, nests tae look for.

Sandy an' yer gran'faither ha'e spent a' their days beside the wid; they played in't tae, an' though they're owre auld tae play in't the same wye as ye play; they still play in the wid, they mak' stories o' the wid. The nicht they were playin' wi' a winter's wid. Wait you till the simmer comes roon, an' they'll tell ye brave, blithe stories o' a *simmer's* wid."

"Mither", he speired, " wis that the wye ye'd a wee lauch on yer face, because ye kent they war jist playin'?"

"Aye," she said, "that wis the wye."

She left him eence he wis in his bed; an' tho' he couldna richt un'erstan' fit she meant, he wis a bittie comforted.

Still, it wis lang or he sleepit, for mannies wi' big, tile hats, and blue lichts keekit in at him through the window. He wished it wis the simmer, for he jist didna like a winter's wid.

The Flowering Currant

THE flowering currant was older than despair. It was almost as old as Mina herself – almost. Mina had lived on earth for six years before she discovered that there was room for the flowering currant to live, too.

The earth in Mina's six-year-old comprehension was the distance between her own room in the town and her grandmother's house. Five miles embraced a world which sloped on one side in wooded breadth, and on the other side in chequered, ever-changing patches of parks to reach the sky which marked the end of the world. But the small brown cottages were dotted safely in the centre of the world, and it was here Mina discovered that the red flowering currant had a being – a shaggy, straggling, dusty bush, from which drooped the wee red flower with a smell that was comforting, and homely and warmly bitter.

The other flowers which made up Mina's posy, wilting on the slow, homeward five-mile walk from her grandmother's house to the room in the close, lost all essence, all identity, by the time they'd reached the unavailing water in the jam-jar. Curious that that loss was effected by nothing other than a desire to hold. The result of a gripping, possessive, clammy hand was but a mess of dry, faded yellows and blues that once were flowers.

The flowering currant was part of the faded mass, but this flower lost freshness without ever losing its essence. Even an hour afterwards, when her mother had doomed the jam-jar and its contents to lie with the ashes in the scaffie's box behind the door, Mina could still smell the flowering currant off the hand that had carried it.

*   *   *   *   *   *   *

With the passing of twenty years, the world grew larger, but time became shorter. Summers that had been a lifetime were now insufficient to contain the days' dargs. Mina had no time to search for the flowering currant, and, though it remained glowing in her mind's depths as the complement to all gardens, she never noticed the dusty, shaggy bush, and the unobtrusive, red flower in any garden she chanced to see.

The seasons changed aspect. They presented no longer wondrous anticipation, infinite variety, secrecy; those rare things are preserved exclusively for childhood.

Mina lived too closely to the seasons to be quite estranged from them. But the tattie flou'er was not now pale foams of heliotrope, masses of white blossoms centred with yellow, but a signal that soon it would be tattie-liftin' time. . . Then the hale warld wad absorb itsel' intae lang, broon dreels, and time wad be counted as a meenit for strauchtenin' yer back ti feel its sairness, faur thocht lost itsel', and only the senses keepit their use *because*, thocht Mina, *they canna dae ither.*

Fan the lang tattie-liftin' days war burnt-smellin' and bricht, the "stages" that war Mina's cam tae end doon far the loch glinted through the trees; syne Mina's een found relief in surprise that there was nae mair dreel but, fair in front o' her, a wud wi' the blowsiness o' full simmer jist awa' fae'd, and yellow rumours o' early autumn ower it; and alow the wud the secretive glimmer o' a loch tryin' sair tae hide itsel'. Mina kent the loch was there. She nivir peered ower the dyke without feelin' the surprise o't and mindin' o' the loch in a book – *a fern-shaded pool come across in dreams.*

But fan the tattie-liftin' mornin's war weet-misted, and the glaured earth keepit the tatties in its cauld clammy grip, and it was gaun up the brae o' the dreels instead o' doon, ilka step gaed farrer fae the loch, and Mina hersel' felt as much pairt o' the tattie park as the broon mools themsel's. Nae that she ivir revealed her deadness. She leuch at the roughness o' the ither tattie-lifters' jokes – she even tell't rougher anes hersel'. Fan the day endit, there was her hoose tae tend till the thocht o' undune tasks cryin' tae be completed in the dark, damp hoose, the realisation that there wad be nae time tae reflect wi' ane's sel' for a meenit, and the morn wad bring mair tattie-acres tae be lifted, make rough jokes a relief. Scum rises without effort, bit reflection bides far ben, and that's a luxury that needs time.

Fan the park tired o' tatties and cried oot for grain, Mina was again absorbed intae'd, forkin' barley; syne helpin' tae thresh it. The park likit eident mortals.

Mina hated that great sloping park with a hatred she could never rightly analyse. It filled her with a tremendous fear. *It's because I want things that I'm bound ti this park. I've got mate, claes, and a hoose, so maybe I dinna need muckle, but tae want is aye mair intense than tae need. I want books, a typewriter, a wee organ tae play tunes on in the winter. I want tae see ither countries; maist o' a' I want time. I'm feart I'm turnin' intae a clod, feart I'll forget the things that dinna touch existence, but that sweeten the core o' livin'.*

It was a windy day in Simmer. The wind tried sair tae haud awa' the rain. Mina lowsin' sheaves on the top o' the threshin'-mill kent aboot the wind. It blew the chaff and yavins wi' roused thrawnness intae her een. The forkers, sair in the een as weel, threw the sheaves up at random hitting her on the face, the feeder tuggit impatiently at the sheaves; naethin' hurt his een ahint protective goggles; the mill itsel' throbbit, relentlessly groaning. The fore-neen wearin' bye was the only slow thing in a space o' hurtlin' yavins and fleein' chaff.

Mina, owre auld tae greet aboot things in her een, found outlet in the anger growin' inside hersel'.

I'm gaein' doon aff this mill. I'm like a frenzied mill masel'. The yavins are bitin' the een awa' fae me. I'll nivir, nivir lowse again!

Mina didna gang doon. Lowsin' at a threshin'-mill is a curious thing; ane's will becomes lost; ane's hands can only stop cutting the sheaves fan the mill stops cryin' oot for them.

The rain stoppit the mill – great, black torrential rain wi' a sting sharper than the wind itsel'.

Mina didna gang straicht hame, tho' hame needed her. The mornin's terrilbleness wanted ootlet. She gaed intae the wud, that wad mak' nae claims on her. She cooried doon in the big sandy hole, feelin' mair elemental than human, and hopit it wad rain forivir.

Lang efter she cam' oot fae the hiddenness. She loupit the dyke. Syne she saw it, jist faur it was likely tae growe – a dusty, stragglin' bush wi' a red flooer. She grasped it wi' her hand and buried her nose in its wetness. It had the same warm, comfortin' smell that she kent fan the warld was jist five miles lang and ended at the side o' the sky. This was the flooer that had hidden in her mind a' the years though she'd nivir seen it since bairnhood.

Mina gaed hamewards wi' wondrous gledness. The park micht tire her again, but it wad nivir fear her ony mair. She kent the years hadna managed tae steal the joy that aince was. It was fan she was supperin' her man that she thocht on't.

I'm awa' tae the wud. There's a flooerin' currant bush there. I henna seen that flooer since I wis a bairn. I thocht it didna growe hereabout. I'm awa' tae bring hame a bit o't.

She reached the wud. There was the sandy hole, and here was the bit dyke doon fae't. But nae sign o' a flooerin' currant bush. She smelt the hand she'd graspit the bush wi'. It still keepit the comfortin', intimate smell o' a flooerin' currant.

Contentment

He was lean, stooping shoulders kept him from being tall, and his hair was a startling combination of the black that glints blue and the white that has nae gray in it. He looked as if he'd niver had tae pass through the "grayin" stage, as the youth had niver left him and age had come tae bide with him. Their generous incongruous crown o black and white bowed in assent til acceptable opinions delivered at the brig, or shook in definite disapproval over local politics voiced and examined by his cronies on the dyke-side auditorium.

"There's nae pleasin' in fowk," he wad say. "Nane. Tak Heaven itsel doun til earth and gie them the freedom o't, and still they'd look for something lackin in't. It's contentment they've lost, and aince ye've lost contentment there's nae eese lookin for't. It's a queer loss, ye niver find it again, it's like . . . ."

His audience was unappreciative. Jeems Sim was mair taen up wi watchin Jock the gowk – Jock, newly promoted fae gowk til scaffie, was sliverin aboot the mou fyles he sweepit the yalla leaves fae anent the dyke. Harry Robb had naethin in his auld bleary een bit a watery licht, a hope for five o'clock and the rattle o the price o a hauf pint in his pooch.

His ain interest was all-absorbing, he niver noticed the lack of interest in ithers. He'd draw a thocht oot fae the deeps o his mind, probe it and explain it til himself, loud eneuch so that he could hear it. The passers-by heard it as weel, heard it so often that only the bairns found novelty in it and gave voice to that novelty:

Wanderin Doddie speakin tae himself
Bit fat he's sayin
Naebody can tell.

"It's like," he fumbled the words ower each ither in his eagerness tae gie a tangible explanation, "it's like bairnhood, contentment. Ye mind aboot fan ye had it, bit ye needna look for't again."

When Belle in the shop gied him his bit cheese she also gied him gratis food for a hale efternoon's thocht: "Awa for your walk, Doddie? Weel, it's graun weather for't, bit och, it's nae seasonable, it's jist nae like Christmas at aa." Wasna that jist proof positive o fat he'd discovered, and kent for the past thirty year? Fowk were born with contentment, bit maist o them grew careless eneuch tae lose it. Syne they spent the rest o their lives lookin for't. Of course they niver found it, it was that lang since they tint it that they'd forgotten fat like it looked.

For instance, Belle wasna wholly pleased with this day that belonged tae winter though spring had creepit intil it three months afore her time and gien Doddie a fey feelin. There was the river, noo – niver in December had Doddie seen the river like fat it was the day. Maybe it was the coloured lichts fae the sky that did it, in late efterneens the sky had a wye whiles o turning red. Bit it wasna that kind o vivid red the day, it had pinkness, the deep yalla pinkness o a salmon past its best, and doon on the sheen, o the dark saft face of the water the sky's colours lay in reflection as bricht in the deeps as awa up abune the cloods. "Like ane o they rich dark paintins in oil," thocht Doddie, "only nae man body could paint like that."

Aa alang the river's bank the feyness byded wi him, walkin in a day o spring that had creepit intil December, as if for mischief. And what mischief! Even summer had pairt in the ploy for, grawin up the dyke, lauchen at the laws that mannies cried naturalists laid doon for themsels, smaa and without smell bit pink and absolute, was ae wild rose.

The hedgerows wi winter's yalla ower them were auld in colour only, the lithe trigness o spring was in their bearin. The very grun aneth his feet was in spring's grip, black and saft and resilient.

The best was yet tae come. Doddie kent the tree at the bend o the river. It was a halting place. The tree hungered tae hae its dwelling on baith banks. Its great roots were embedded on this bank, its lean off-shooting branches arched clean ower the river in an effort tae touch the ither side.

It wis a tree that was niver lonely. Ilka day Doddie wad lean against the dyke and watch them that loved the tree. Lang afore he reached it he kent they'd keepit tryst. He kent by their bikes wi the boxes o undelivered messages in front o them, for even at fourteen and earnin seventeen-and-six a week, they hadna outgrown the tree. They took lang cuts, and some grocer's time, tae swoop doon like raiders and reclaim their ain territory. Syne, wi the wee loons' rope, they'd fulfil the tree's ain ambition and swing fae this side til the t'ither. Doddie was their only watcher.

For he had nane o the auld's jealousy – or maybe waur, their mere tolerance – o youth. He was grateful til the young for being sae. He wad hae clappit their tousled heids, if he hadna kent they'd resent it, oot o sheer gratitude for their youth. Instead, he keepit an eye on the quiverin rope and its burden, and wad cry oot: "Watch yersels, loonies, the branch michtna haud!"

And though some wifie was keepit waitin for her errands, in the contrary wye loons hiv they didna quite forget their status as wage-earners, and objecting to being cad "loonies" they'd cry back in outrage, "Sez you, grandfaither."

For aa that, Doddie wad stan guardian at the tree till the last loon mindit he owed the grocer a duty. . .

Fan Doddie turned the bend, the gowden colours sprang at him; he likit broom best, it was deeper in hue and threw its smell awa generously – still, whins gave their yallas til a December day. Up abune the whins the hoose stood on a slope. Its windows watched the river richt fae the brig til Laverock Hill. The hoose was anither haltin place.

Queer tae think that Bill Chisholm biggit that hoose for himself, forbye haein twa butcher's shops and a van that gaed roon the country. Doddie had kent Bill fine in the days fan he wasna a butcher bit jist a loon caad "Bubblie Bokie" because his nose was aye rinnin.

Doddie envied Bill naethin bit the hoose. He aften winnered if Bill iver lookit oot and saw the ploys aneth the tree that was niver lonely, or saw the river alowe wi colours fae the sky; bit maybe no, wi twa shops and a van a butcher wadna hae muckle time tae stan and look. Ambition realised maun fair be satisfactory, bit fat a time is lost realisin it – and time, like contentment, disna come back again.

The river's glint wound roon tae lose itsel ahint Laverock hill. Some day Doddie was gaun tae follow it on and on till he cam til its beginning. He kent this bit o't that weel that he wantit tae see fat gave birth til't. He'd hae tae start early though, for wha kent the distance til the birth o a river?

It wadna be the morn, he had tae gang for his pension then. Queer hoo the pension workit the week oot. "Jist like some provident natural law," thocht Doddie.

On the last nicht o the week he'd aye jist one and sixpence neat, fowerpence ha'penny for a loaf, fowerpence ha'penny for his cheese ration, and ninepence for his bed in the lodgin-hoose.

May Melody

Chris was fifteen, and though she had noticed several Mays pass over Inchettle, she had never really *seen* them. She saw this May only because it stared at her in big headlines from the centre page of the daily paper, which Father, out of long habit, read between the time of finishing his porridge and waiting for his tea.

"Maytime Customs." It started with a poem – at least, Chris was still young enough to have the idea that everything that rhymed was poetry.

> *Ah, 'tis like a tale of olden time,*
> *Long, long ago,*
> *When the world was in its golden prime*
> *And Love was lord below.*
> *Every vein of earth was dancing*
> *With the Spring's new wine,*
> *'Twas the pleasant time of flowers*
> *When I met you, love of mine.*
> *Ah! Some spirit sure was straying*
> *On that day*
> *When I met you, sweet, a-maying*
> *In that merry, merry May.*

Chris read it once, undaunted by Father's grunts of disapproval. His dislike of "fowk reading over ma shooder" was deep-rooted. Syne she read it again, and without being conscious of having learned it, imprinted it on her mind.

It was more than poetry, it was music! Chris, swirling the porridge plates round in the soap suds, *made* it music. She could never recapture the same tune twice, but the words kept singing. Father's voice – "For God's sake, if ye're gaun tae sing, sing richt and nae scraich awa there! That's nae singin, it's domineerin!" – silenced the words, but the melody remained.

When she ran out to hang the dish-towel over the fence, Chris stood still to absorb the first May she'd ever really seen. The purple lilac-tree, drenched and heavy with sweetness; the white lilac-tree, fragile, foam-like; the sticky scentedness of beech trees; velvet dusty-millers shedding their crimson along the borders; the visible world rich and full and sweet-smelling; and over to the east where the sky was red, the unknown city lay. This was the painted May that Chris was always to keep; it seemed to impart its very colour into her imagination, its sweetness into her thoughts.

She packed her schoolbag automatically. Strange how her essay on the French Revolution had seemed so good and so important last night; today it didn't matter. Robespierre, Danton and Marat were only names, and names of dead men at that, but this was May and real and sweet, its sweetness hurting Chris physically.

She washed her face with loving carefulness. Having once read that lemon makes the skill beautiful, she rescued a wizened piece from the scullery ledge. Her own faith worked the miracle. She *felt* beautiful.

Half defiantly – for total defiance, she knew, set Mother's back up – she broached the subject of her Sunday coat. She felt curiously angry wi Mither, who looked so old and ordinary, dully asking for an explanation that, when given, she probably wadna understand.

"Far ails ye at yer school coat? Yer ither coat's the only ane ye hiv for Sunday, mind,"

The pent-up hatred of her school coat found vent in Chris's tumbled reply: "I jist hate ma school coat! It's ower lang and wide for me. Some bits o't are green and the faded bits are blue. It's Mary's old coat. I like ma Sunday coat because it's ma ain, it's neat and fits me richt. Fan I quarrel wi Jess Christie and the ither quines they cry *Mary's coat! Ye wear yer sister's claes!* They've niver seen me richt dressed."

Mither, who was a loving observer under her oldness and ordinariness, watched Chris disappear through Inchettle woods in the coat that was "neat and fits richt", watched with the resignation that whiles enters all mothers' eyes.

Nothing dimmed the glow of that May day for Chris. The classroom door was left open to let the sweetness and warmth filter in. Chris remained bound up in her own secrecy though the dominie's voice meandered through decades of past things – the Israelites crossing the Red Sea; Mark Antony's oration over Caesar's body; figures of speech – alliteration, metaphor; Political Revolution in France, Industrial Revolution in Britain; equations, parallelograms. Each phase of that day's lessons touched her mind with its own small, distinct clarity, but in her heart Chris was unresponsive. If she could have given words to her thoughts, she would have said, "I'm ower auld to be interested in school noo. I'm fifteen, and I'm bonny."

Homeward bound on the pathway through Inchettle woods, Chris was still lost in her dreams. Wull Watt found her, Wull who was going to Gordon's College after the summer, whom Chris admired because theorems never flummoxed him.

"Jump on ma back step, Chris," was the greeting of the lad who had never before, on all the homeward treks, shown such chivalry. Her new instinct told her that a Sunday coat doesn't show to advantage on the back of a bike.

"Weel, gie's yer books, I'll cairry them." They walked in silence. The spell broke when they reached Inchettle Quarry. He clattered his bike against a tree. Curiously dumb and shy, they looked at each other.

All that the day had brought surged upwards in Chris's mind – the painful morning joy; the sweetness still lingering over the wood; the Sunday coat; the assurance that she was bonny; the queer look on Wull's face; their aloneness in the wood. It all blended together.

> *Ah, 'tis like a tale of olden time*
> *Long long ago,*
> *When the world was in its golden prime*
> *And Love was lord below.*

With it came a blinding awareness. Chris snatched her books from Wull's hand: "I'm jist feart, Wull!"

Syne her running figure was lost in Inchettle woods.

Pilgrimage

THE wood was smaller in its new reality than it was in the picture Phemie's mind had so jealously preserved. So Phemie, at thirty, preferred to look at the wood across an expanse of twenty years. She saw it more clearly from the distance. For a brief moment it stood before her starkly – as it was – just a scraggy copse on a bare hillock. But, since she was on a pilgrimage, long planned, eagerly looked forward to, Phemie, like all pilgrims, discovered that what *is* doesn't matter, what *was* is absolute.

*   *   *   *   *   *   *

Where the wood slopes to its highest point there grows an immense beech tree. Forty years of bairns have cut their names on that tree; the spirit of the Orphanage in the hollow below pervades the whole wood.

Fancy stole up there to be exercised, grievances escaped up there to be aired. Strange tales were told amongst its trees; some of them alien to the wholesomeness of a wood.

It was so easy and comforting to lie on the warm, humming grass and recall the hungers of former days in the sure knowledge of supper at six – and plenty of it.

And whiles, encompassed with very safety, it was not difficult to look backwards benevolently and draw rose-mists over former sordidness. It was within the power of childhood to transform shameful, past episodes into sagas of a golden age. Neither the wood, nor the listeners, were ever certain if the tale being told came from actuality or imagination. Nor was the issue important. A tale is a tale.

It was Phemie's own desire to cap a tale which was the cause of still-remembered horror. Phemie was one of the orphans who found it easier to draw her tales from imagination than from truth. When one is ten, truth is still near enough to hurt, and too secret to be shared.

Phemie found imagination could hurt, too, but not at that moment when Andrew and Chrissie and Pete sat hugging their knees and asking for a story – "a real ane!"

"A real ane" was taken to be one that was true.

"Aince," said the story-teller, "I threw my mother intil a big river. She floundered aboot in the water, syne sank till the bottom. She bed there for a week, and ae day she came hame as dry's a bane. She said aince yer richt alow the water it's jist the same as on earth, only nae fowk bides there, bit jist fishes that can flee."

The tale that was "as true as death" troubled the teller. Phemie herself began to believe it. She wanted to be absolved from the horror of a deed that now she wasn't sure whether or not she had committed. *Dear God*, she would say into herself when the suspense became unbearable, *I dinna think I threw my mither intil a big river. I jist said it for a story. Bit if I did throw her in, I'm sorry.*

*   *   *   *   *   *   *

But none had so much knowledge of the wood as the eleven ducks and one drake. Phemie, to whom was entrusted the care of the ducks, acquired knowledge of the wood solely through the waywardness of her ducks.

Dilly! Dilly! was her cry on the night she lost the ducks and found the wild pansies. Clumps of broom bushes hid their surprise well, and to Phemie, who was not looking for surprise, the hollow of solid purple with yellow eyes was wonder given meaning. The spirit of a miser who has secret wealth entered her: *They're my pansies! I found them first! I'll nivir tell a soul!*

The home-taking of the ducks ceased to be a duty and became a vocation. Phemie was no longer annoyed when the drake cajoled his wives to *bide awee yet* in the precincts of the burn. The reason was simple. "You" (ducks and drake) "and me kens far the wild pansies growe."

When the wild pansies faded out of all but secrecy, the rowans bloomed in their stead. Not quite in the pansies' stead, the rowans were too profuse ever to be a secret.

"Hame" was strangely remembered and interwoven with Orphanage life. Phemie completed much of the weaving in this wood. She viewed the time between "here" and "hame" with urgency. There was so much to be taken from here to "hame", so much that was novel to "hame". Phemie sometimes felt terror lest she'd forget to take all the things "hame".

The pansy-discovery was one of the things. It could not be included in the once-weekly, censored letter. There was so much that could not be included in that letter, and so much that didn't matter made up the letter's contents.

The rowans were also of things to be preserved; the broom, too, when the time came for it to burst into flame, and the old twigs stretching untidily along the dykeside, allowing none but the ducks to waddle through their gnarled intricacy. The twigs, while having goodwill towards the ducks, had none towards Phemie, but caught her legs in their vicious grips and writhed and crackled round her when she emerged with the eggs as though they protested against her taking what lawfully belonged to the ducks.

The cry of *Dilly! Dilly!* became varied with the cry of *Treeste! Treeste!* For the two cows were added to Phemie's responsibilities. Phemie never understood the cows as well as she understood the ducks. She almost understood them when she was well behind them with a stick; but when, on occasion, the cows, in their deliberate way, would turn completely round to examine Phemie, then even slight understanding fled, and Phemie followed it.

The cows had access to the wood only for a wee while in the summer, but, when they munched the wood's grass, Andrew and Phemie found their friendship threatened through Andrew's chance remark:

"We're gaun tae play in the coos' wud the nicht."

"It's the ducks' wud!" Phemie protested. "The ducks bide in't a' the time."

"The coos are bigger and cost mair money", Andrew argued.

"Ay," said Phemie, bit there's only twa coos, and there's eleven ducks an' the drake."

The "Ducks' Wud" was established and such it remained.

*   *   *   *   *   *   *

The wood saw words become deeds. Andrew would catch the burn's water in walls of mud. He was a generous engineer, he built not only a dam for himself, but was overseer and assistant in building the dams of his smaller companions.

The sole payment that Andrew ever demanded for his labours was that only himself should be allowed to kick down the dams and release the water.

Building up was never as joyous as "knockin' doon". Delighted shouts rent the air when the water released from captivity rushed down the hillside.

Then the ducks would come to revel in the drookit mud.

The wood that doesn't know of the existence of "Cowboys and Indians" has missed its vocation. The Ducks' Wud knew the species well. When Nell the collie was still in her youth, she took active part in the Cowboys' raids against the Indians. Nell became a horse. Pete called her Tony, "because Tom Mix in the picture-hoose at hame has a great horse cried Tony!"

Nell never got used to her new name; she remained Nell. Nor would she ever allow aspirant riders to mount her. Andrew viewed her lack of cooperation philosophically!

"She's a damned nuisance aye barkin' roon oor hidie places an' giein' the show awa; but she's jist a dog, so she can be the riderless horse."

The "riderless horse" understood rabbits and crows far better than she understood Cowboys and Indians, though sometimes, when she'd chased all the crows to the sanctuary of the tree-tops and barked all the rabbits into their burrows, Nell, with nothing more exciting in view, would take part in a struggle between a Cowboy and an Indian. She was a neutral combatant. She bit the legs and tugged at the breeks of baith the battlers.

The quines came in for their share of patronage when Cowboys and Indians held sway in the wood.

"Ye can be Great Chief for a whilie," coaxed Andrew on a day when Phemie found daisy-chaining more attractive than whooping through the wood. Phemie grasped opportunity:

"I'll only play if ye cut my name oot on the beech tree; ye aye promised ye wad dae't."

Thus it was that Phemie, who gave the wood its name, had her own name added to the tree that kept the names of all the Orphanage bairns.

*   *   *   *   *   *   *

Strange it was no longer a scraggit copse that confronted Phemie. It was a wood vast enough to hold all secrecy, all illusions, a wood she'd known intimately twenty years ago. Nothing was lost. As she walked down the slopes, she could see all the bairns – Andrew, Chrissie, Bertha, Frank . . . something of their immortality was locked in the wood. She knew that, because Pete was killed at St Valery, but she saw him gesticulating twenty years away; she heard his voice:

"Come on you anes! Last doon fae the wud is a hairy worm!"

Radio Plays

Apples Be Ripe

An impression of an Aberdeenshire Autumn, written and introduced by Jessie Kesson

A stretch o' sober dyke guards a' the corn
Like some auld farrant chiel wi' haudin' his gowd-haired quines,
Fae burstin' wi' a gaudie ecstasy.
But aye they shak' their heavy tresses
And reeshle wi' their lauchter – secretly.
Syne, farther on, flauntin' the dyke intae obscurity
The hips and haws afire
Gleamin' wi' rain.

This Autumn nicht's put blindness on tae me.
I'll nivir see the lang-stane dyke again,
In Spring and Simmer, aye, in Winter tae,
I'll see the lauchin' corn and the reid hips
Weet wi' the rain. [1]

<u>Narrator:</u>
It's Autumn at Clayfaulds. We felt it coming: now we can see it. Some things are best forgotten. The wood that used to cover the whole breadth o' Clayfauld's hill is one of those things. We hinna yet got used to what the war did to our wood. In country places like Clayfaulds every single bit o' landscape is familiar tae us in a' its aspects; city fowk on the other hand can spend their whole lives in one street and still never be really intimate wi' that street. It's different at Clayfaulds – on the day that I looked oot and saw nothing left o' the hill wood but some antrin stumps; a queer, physical pain went through me. It was as if I'd looked on the face o' an auld frien' and found it mutilated.

That was why we thought Autumn was slow in comin' this year. For, when the wood covered the hill, Autumn seemed tae come suddenly like a bricht, blindin' flash. Ae day we'd look up and the wood wad still be in its Summer green, syne the next day when we looked up, the wood smouldered red and yellow like a muckle furnace. But the seasons didna stop coming when the Forestry Commission cut down the wood for essential timber. That most Autumn-like o' trees still flourishes here and there at Clayfaulds. A poet once described the cherry tree as "the loveliest of trees." **2** *I* think there's nothing to touch the rowan tree. It's aye lovely even when it's got neither bloom nor berry. The interlacing pattern of its leaves perpetuates delicate beauty.

Song: Lady Nairne's *Rowan Tree:*

> *Oh! Rowan Tree Oh Rowan Tree!*
> *Thou'lt aye be dear to me,*
> *Entwined thou art wi mony ties,*
> *O' hame and infancy.*
> *Thy leaves were aye the first o' spring,*
> *Thy flow'rs the simmer's pride;*
> *There was nae sic a bonny tree*
> *In a' the countryside*

> *Oh! Rowan Tree!*

The difference between the city and Clayfaulds in the Autumn cam' hame to me last week. I stood in Union Street, Aberdeen, at the rush hour. The whole length and breadth o' its pavements were black wi' fowk – hundreds o' fowk. All of them unknown to me – all of them in a hurry. The sight filled me wi' a strange panic. There was something terrible in their vast numbers, something ruthless in their haste. At Clayfaulds we a' ken each other and we hurry slowly, slowly. But here I stood in the heart o' Aberdeen, dazed, jostled and buffeted by the rushing mass. And though I was only in town for the day, and hame was but ten short miles awa' I felt homesick for the slow serenity o' Clayfaulds. I thocht . . . . "It's a queer thing, it's hairst-time at Clayfaulds, and nae business or work in the world is so urgent and essential as hairst. It's a sort o' fundamental thing like eating and sleeping. And yet for a' its urgency the fowk winna be rushin' at Clayfaulds the mad wye they're rushin' in the street. They'll be makin' in-roads tae the corn parks; slowly and methodically. The youngest orra-loon will be whistlin' because it's his very first hairst and he hasna haen time tae tire yet. It's Autumn there at Clayfaulds ten miles awa' but ye'd never ken that it's Autumn here in Union Street . . . "My train of thought was broken by an irate wifie pushing her pram agin my shins in an effort to pass. "Some fowk", she said loudly to her companion – "Some fowk hiv a' day tae stan' an' glower so that they nivir think ither fowk might be in a hurry. They need a lot o' room as weel. Ye'd think they war the only anes that peyed rates an' taxes for the use o' the pavement! Or maybe the poor thing's jist in a trance."

The angry wifie's attempt at sarcasm hit the mark. I really was "a poor thing jist in a trance". Cities have a paralysing effect on me. I was only myself again, and happy, when the 'bus rattled toward Clayfaulds in the dusk o' the Autumn nicht.

Verse by John Drinkwater:

> *And now the valleys that upon the sun*
> *Broke from their opal veils are veiled again.*
> *And the last light upon the wolds is done,*
> *And silence falls on flocks and fields and men.*
> *And black upon the night I watch my hill,*
> *And the stars shine, and all again is still* [3]

But Clayfaulds welcomes the eident Autumn days, the lengthening lamp-lit nights. Summer brought its ain distractions but it's Autumn that maks Clayfaulds sma' and intimate. In the gloom o' ony o' its scattered kitchens no topic is so important as hairst weather on a September nicht.

Farm worker: That mist's still comin' doon; the hill's near aboot happit wi' it. We'll hae anither drookit day the morn. Aye, we will that. If only the rain wad haud awa' till we win through wi' the leadin'.

Wife: *(resignedly)*. Weel, there's anither day comin'. Ye've worried aboot the mist on that hill for forty hairsts noo and it's nivir yet rained sae sair that ye didna get the hairst in in time.

Farm worker: Ach Fie! I ken fine we've aye gotten't in in time! It's jist that I like tae see a' the grain parks lyin' stubble fan September ends.

<u>Wife</u>: Ye'd tae wait till ye was born so ye can surely contain yersel wi' patience till a gweed leadin' day turns up. Ye micht hand me doon the socks that's airin' on the rack; the heels are clean oot o' them. I jist canna keep ye in socks fan it's a wet hairst.

<u>Narrator</u>: That's Clayfaulds and its fowk. We were born wi' the instinct that hairst is the climax o' oor labours. We share this instinct wi' the poets. Maybe poets and country fowk aye find the fundamental things simple tae understand.

<u>Verse by John Drinkwater</u>

> *I see the wagons move along the rows*
> *Of ripe and summer-breathing clover flower,*
> *I see the lissom husbandman who knows*
> *Deep in his heart the beauty of his power,*
> *As, lithely pitched, the full-heaped fork bids on*
> *The harvest home. I hear the rickyard fill*
> *With gossip as in generations gone,*
> *While wagon follows wagon from the hill.*
> *I think how, when our seasons all are sealed*
> *Shall come the unchanging harvest from the field.* [4]

<u>Narrator</u>: Some old customs still survive even in the age of the atom bomb. Change comes slowly tae the parish kirk at Clayfaulds, and so we a' ken the hymn Mr Forsyth will cry oot for the Harvest Thanksgiving Service. We've sung it for thirty harvests noo.

<u>Parish Kirk Bells, followed by hymn:</u>

> *O Lord of heaven and earth and sea,*
> *To thee all praise and glory be;*
> *How shall we show our love to thee,*
> *Who givest all?*

<u>Narrator</u>: When the last waggon-load reaches the stackyard Clayfaulds prepares its barn for the Harvest Home. Clayfaulds younger generation can "swing it" and use American "patter" wi' the best o' their city cousins. But on the nicht o' the Harvest Home

"swing" and "patter" have no place in Clayfaulds' barns. On this nicht ye can catch a glimpse o' an Aberdeenshire that's fast disappearin'. Ye can hear the accents o' a doric that's dying out.

Accordion playing an Eightsome reel

Voice: *(Jokingly)* Man Harry, if ye'd steppit through Burndyke's stooks as swalk as I saw ye steppin't oot tae come here the nicht Burndyke's hairst wad hae been in lang syne.

Harry: *(Laughingly)* Aye, and if ye'll jist put mair pith intae that concertina thing ye'll see me steppin' oot swalker still.

General jovial agreement: That's the idea, Harry! We're a' supple in the joints fan we're oot o' the yoke. Come on fowks, it's lowsin' time. Let's a' join in.

Volume of Eightsome reel increases and ends after a few bars.

Voice *(Winded – distant)* That was hot work! As hard as ony day's work. Fit aboot you younger anes singin' a song till we aulder fowk get oor wind back? There's naething like an eightsome tae mak a lad feel his age.

Voice: Ach, ye're nae auld, Jimmy! Jist sixty fower, yer bit a laddie yet.

Other voices joining in: Richt, Davie, play up! A sang we a' ken. Come on, May.

Song – "Johnnie Sangster." Accordeon, chorus by all.

> *O' a' the seasons o' the year*
> *When we maun work the sairest,*
> *The harvest is the only time,*
> *And yet it is the rarest,*
> *We rise as seen as mornin' licht,*
> *Nae craters can be blither*
> *We buckle on oor finger steels*
> *And follow oot the scyther.*

For you, John-nie, you John-nie
You, Johnnie Sangster
I'll trim the gavel o' my sheaf
For you're the gallant bandster. [5]

Narrator: The hours have flown past. The hairst rejoicing is over. The barn is silent; the auld homely smell o' oilcake and foosty smell o' dust creeps back to it. The wind twangs through its broken panes. Autumn is coming to its close everywhere – except at Clayfaulds, whaur the seasons nivir end. This nicht Clayfaulds rejoiced for the harvest of 1946. In less than a month Clayfauld's horseman will be ploughing the soil for the harvest of 1947.

Poem by Thomas Hardy

Only a man harrowing clods
In a slow silent walk
With an old horse that stumbles and nods
Half asleep as they stalk.

Only thin smoke without flame
From the heaps of couch grass
Yet this will go onward the same
Though dynasties pass. [6]

Highland Spring

An old Highland woman living in Aberdeenshire lets her memory take her back to a Spring forty years ago on the Black Isle

[Incidental music ; Greig's "Spring"]

<u>John Beaton:</u> So this is faur ye've got till, mither? Fine div ye ken that ye shouldna be sittin' oot in this damp porch. I'm sure there's a mair comfortable chair in the hoose tae sit in than here.

<u>Mrs Beaton:</u> *(with a Highland accent)* Aye . . . . maybe more comfortable places, John. . . . but it's here that *I* like to sit . . . .I can see the woods from here . . .the Craigievar woods, and the hills, . . . and och it's the first fine day we've had since long . . .and I was just minding that it would be Spring in . . . . .

<u>John Beaton:</u> *(Interrupting with verve)* I ken! I ken! Ye've got that hankerin' look i' yer e'e again. Ye're aye content eneuch wi' Aiberdeenshire fan it's wintertime bit as sune as Spring comes ye growe restless an' fashous . . . and it's aye the same story . . . the Black Isle, the bonny Black Isle as ye aye speak o'. . .*(Teasingly)* . . .surely mither, efter spen'in' forty years o' yer life in Aiberdeenshire ye're nae *still* hankerin' for the Black Isle!

<u>Mrs Beaton:</u> No, not hankering for it . . . . .. I'm just minding about it . . . ... just minding ..

<u>John Beaton:</u> *(Still teasingly)* Ye've got a lang memory, mither. I thocht ye'd hae forgotten that sic a place as the Black Isle existed – weel, weel, I'll hae tae awa' and feed the calvies noo . . . .Mind, dinna ye sit owre lang in that porch, the dampness comes doon that quick.

<u>Mrs Beaton:</u> *(Speaking to herself)* Don't be fashing yourself about me, John Beaton. Because I'm an old woman you're thinking I've got one foot in the grave . . . . *(with a chuckle)* . . . but indeed I'm more alive than yourself that is my son. . . . . I can sit back in this

old, damp porch and see my whole life. . . and O. . . it's wonderful seeing . . . . for when you're old and look back you don't see the ordinary, drab things that made up your life . . . . .it's queer you just see the joyful, glinting things . . . and I'm not in Aberdeenshire at all . . . . I'm four miles east from Cromarty . . . and it's Spring . . . . a Spring forty years away. . .

Reader: Glen Udale! O Glen Udate!
           High the sorrel there and the sweet fragrant grasses!
           It would be well if I were listening now to where
           In Glen Udale the sun shines and the cool west wind passes
           Glen Udale of the grasses!   [1]

Mrs Beaton: It was the tinkers who took the first sign of Spring to the hills above Udale Bay. We knew that winter was over and done with the moment we heard their carts rattling up the moor-tracks. They came in swarms across the ferry from Tain and Invergordon. And they were a welcome sight! They brought a touch of colour and humour . . . and their own inevitable music. . .

[Distant tinker piper plays "Road to the Isles", against clatter of tins]

Tinker Boy: Hiv ye a copper for the piper, lady? He's ma faither . . . and ma mither's at ma back . . .she'll tell yer fortune for you . . .she can tell . .

Tinker Woman: *(Whiningly, reproachfully to boy)* If ye bother the nice lass, Colin, I'll paralyse ye stiff . . .but surely a bonnie lass like yersel' will cross my hand wi' silver. . . I'll tell ye a fine fortune. . . (angrily). . . Colin! Ye monkey's image. . . if ye trail that rabbit skins on the ground I'll leave a MacPhee's mark on ye!

Tinker Boy: A'm no' trailin' them! They're fa'in'.

["Road to the Isles" comes nearer, louder]

Tinker Woman: The dogs wull tear the skins. . . lift them, ye de'il's breed! Lift them or I'll brak yer heid! *(Whiningly again)* Come on lass, a fine fortune's yours just for a tanner! . . .Och well, then, ye can surely spare a maskin' o' tea? Or just a pucklie sugar for hansel? *(Angrily again)* Come on, Donald – come on, Colin; there's damn all here but Hieland pride an' hunger!

[Music and clatter fade in distance.]

<u>Mrs Beaton:</u> And in April the grounds of Udale House would be turning yellow with the primroses . . .so thick they were under the beech trees. I could smell them long before I saw them. . . spicy to the smell . . .velvet and dusty to the touch. And down below the house the Newhall Woods stretched like a great, green shadow. . .

<u>Reader</u>   O woods of Newhall I can hear the singing
        Of the west wind among the branches green
        And the leaping and laughing of cool waters springing
        And my heart aches for all that has been.
        For all that has been, my Home, all that has been.[2]

<u>Mrs Beaton:</u> All of my childhood, and a great part of my girlhood is left behind in Newhall Woods. A wood is like a woman; it has so many aspects .. .you seldom get to know it. But *I* knew my wood in Spring .. . its beech trees sticky and sweet smelling; its thrushes so unmusical, but *so* willing to sing . . . its shadows moving with the Spring winds, and its hollows so deep and dark .. .and the foosty, old smell that aye lingers over a wood . . . . the slopes where the young brackens sprang up fresh and green . . . and where the hyacinths grew . . . the hyacinths . . . . . I was nine when I found them. I wasn't looking for them, and the surprise of them is a joy that has stayed with me for fifty years. They grew at the foot of a hollow, so many of them that I thought the hollow itself was deep blue. They were thick and wet, and when I pressed my face amongst them they smelt clean and sharp . . .their cold wetness took the breath from me. Because I was a bairn I was possessive . . . I thought "They're my hyacinths . . .I found them first . . . I'll never tell a soul! " And I didn't . . .till now . . .   .

<u>Reader:</u>   In a hidden wood a blue flower grows
        It is the flower of dream. Who holds it

Is never old.
It is the flower of forgetfulness; and oblivion
Is youth.
Breathing it, flame is not empty air,
Dust is not cold
Lift it, and there is no memory of sorrow
Or any ruth.
The grey monotone of the low sky is filled with light
The dim, terrible, impalpable lie wears the raiment of truth.
I will breathe thy clean, sharp breath O pale blue flower,
And then . . . and then. . . nothing shall take me unaware.[3]

Mrs Beaton: Because I loved that wood as a child I had no fear of it when I was a young girl; on moonlit nights I would walk through it to get to Killen quicker. . . . for the young walk quickly towards happiness and a ceilidh in Helen Cameron's house always meant happiness.

Helen Cameron: Och it's yourself, m'eudail! Bless you! Rory's after coming, and Willie Di's here and we're expecting Seonaid; and it's a grand night we'll have together.

Voice I: *(Teasingly)* Well Mairi, what was the row you were making in Newhall Wood the night when we were passing?

Voice II: Come now, where are you hiding the lad? It was Kenny that was in it, wasn't it?

Helen Cameron: The lassie won't want to tell you who the lad was.

Voice II: Whoever it was, Mairi, you're fairly blushing over him.

(Laughter)

Voice I (Elderly) Aye but wait you, Mairi, wait till you're my age and you'll find that love is like kale – grand in the flavour o' its first fire – but not so good when it's reheated.

(General laughter)

Voice II: *(Emphatically)* No! don't you be heeding him, Mairi! Love's like the whisky that he's got well hidden at Killen – it's the better with the keeping. Come on, Catriona will sing to us. Come on, Catriona.

Sings in English verse of "Arise and Follow Love": others join in chorus.

> When summer's on the mountain and green the glen,
> And heather-bells are greeting the sun again,
> The town of men forsaking, our road we will be taking,
> To where our hearts are waiting, mo nighean donn.
>
> And if there come a grey day to make me sad,
> Mo nighean donn beside me will make me glad,
> With charm for aye enduring, her loving and her luring,
> Bring joy to stay with me and mo nighean donn.
>
> Chorus Rise and follow love, mo nighean donn,
>   Rise and follow love, mo nighean donn,
>   Music from the homeland, sure, I'm hearing,
>   Rise and follow love, mo nighean donn.

Reader: Moonlight and early spring frost make a wood magically beautiful. . . and when I would be walking home after a ceilidh through Newhall Woods the frost would be hanging like silver cobwebs on the branches of the trees. I could never resist pulling my fingers through the shining webs.

(Interlude: Greig's 'Spring')

(Wistfully) there was nothing bleak about the Black Isle. It hadn't the bare dreichness of some parts of Aberdeenshire. . . it was a mellow, kindly land. The couth white cottages of Cromarty seemed to huddle together for comfort. . . . the firth, grey enough in winter, was sapphire-blue in Spring. The windows of the cottages of Invergordon across the Firth glinted red and blue in the sunlight. .

.. the lands around Tain sloped like a huge patchwork quilt – green grazing pasture, brown ploughed parks, and old Ewan . . . Killen's shepherd. . . bent and brown, winding his sheep along the narrow, twisting road; and even at the risk of missing the ferryboat – if Ewan was in the mood to tell the tale, tho' you'd heard it fifty times before – he'd tell you again how Bastan his collie once swam across the Cromarty Firth in the wake of the boat that was carrying Ewan. He was like a child – he never altered the wording of his tale. He always ended it by spitting and saying – 'Mother of God! She did! She did an' all: Bastan herself swam every inch of the Cromarty Firth.' Och, and high up on the slopes of Udale when spring was still bringing twilight the lights would twinkle from the boats on the firth – and on a Sunday evening the men would be singing the psalms, and you could hear every word drifting landwards on a quiet night.

(Psalm ((in harmony) eg 'Kilmarnock')

John Beaton: *(With annoyance)* Mercy, mither! Aye here yet? It's near suppertime an' the rain's been dingin' on this past hour. Hoo did ye nae gang inside fan it cam on? Ye're awfu' – aye forgettin'.

Mrs Beaton: Bit I wasn't forgetting, John – I was only remembering. . .

(Fade out on Greig's "Spring".)

Over Lendrum

[The parts of Helen and Storyteller to be played by the same person]

Autumn. Recollected in tranquillity

Country   Faint countryside station sounds

Porter *(chanting sing song)* Change here for Lendrum! Change here for Lendrum! Change here for Lendrum!

Male Voice Somewhere are places lonely and forgot
          Save by the clouds and early rush of wings
          That, year by year, each hour by hours are shot
          With changing beauty and amazing springs.
          And Autumn flecked with leaves and deep and brown.
          And, in that Autumn, October tumbling down
          Makes its great sounds of fullness in the night.
          High hilled and lost, but now recalled again.
          Rivers that ran from misty rain to rain.
          And cooled our lips when they were young with thirst.

Country Station sounds again

Porter *(still sing song)*
    . . . . For Lendrum! For Lendrum! For Lendrum!

Storyteller If you were born and bred in the parish of Clova, as I was, you became aware of the nearest city of Lendrum long before you are aware of Clova itself, at all. That may be because Clova eventually finds its way to Lendrum. For work, for further education, for entertainment. You feel that life doesn't begin for you till you have gone to Lendrum. Or the reason may even go deeper than that. Clova, being a small howe, cradled in Leuchar's hills, is rocked to the tune of every echo. And *this*, the most repeated tune, becomes the best loved.

Distant station sounds,

Porter Change here for Lendrum! ... Change here for Lendrum ... For Lendrum.....

Storyteller Change here for Lendrum. That instruction was always henceforth to indicate some exciting place winding away from familiar landmarks. And the people who obeyed the instruction were henceforth also always to prove the same kind of people. Young teenagers armed with the badges and the sober Latin mottos of the nearest city's Grammar Schools. And frequently disarmed by fits of the giggles. Women with bulging string bags and outlandish accents. The odd commercial traveller with his brief case, hs hat clinging to his head by a miracle. And I-know-all-the-change-here-for dumps in the world resignation on his face. But that was henceforth. On this late afternoon of early October, the village folk of Clova were kept waiting for their milk, while I absorbed the station. Knowing that I, too, would soon be changing here for Lendrum. I had just got my first job, and success distorted my perceptions. Troyed within the limited landmarks of Clova for sixteen years, I willed my mind to take wings to the larger liberty of Lendrum. But yet, I seemed rooted in Clova.

(Station noises. A crate of fowls bemoaning their desertion on the platform. Chatter. Carriage doors banging.)

Porter All tickets please. All tickets please. All tickets.....

Girl *(impatiently)* Look slippy, Sandy! It's in yer pooch! *(Explanatory to porter)* It's Sandy Mair, Jimmy . He's got a season.

Porter *(lugubriously. Unenchanted by this information)* All tickets please. All tickets.....

Girl. *(increased impatience)* In yer ither pooch, ye Gowk! Och it is so.
(Train leaves)

Country. Group. Near. In greeting to storyteller

1st Boy. Aye Helen. You're ahint wi yer milk the nicht, surely?

Helen *(who is also story teller)* We war late in milkin'. The mill's comin' the morn.

Sandy Are ye tae be threshin' fae the stook, then?

Helen Aye.

1st Boy Auld Beanlie's Mill, or the Government Mill?

Helen Auld Beanlie's.

Sandy. He'll tak a night to back yon ric ma tic in o yer park.

1st Boy. He'll be cursin like Billy-o.

2nd Boy. *(Mimics Auld Beanlie)* Haud her gaun. Haud her gaun! God be here, she's rinnin like a train.

Sandy. *(continues and adds to mimicry)* She'll knock the guts oot o herself if ye dinna haud the oats intil her. Haud her gaun. Haud her gaun.

(All dissolve with laughter except Girl, still trying to retain City School accent and attitude)

Girl. I don't think you're one bit funny, Sandy Mair!

Sandy. *(snort)* Ye wadna!!

(They dissolve in laughter again out of contrariness)

1st boy. Kingorth's started. Look! There's Simmie on the binder.

Shouts in greeting. Aye Simmie!

2nd Boy. They've got a new tractor.

<u>Sandy.</u> We're getting ane after the hairst.

<u>Girl.</u> *(Getting her own back)* You were getting one last hairst. And the hairst before that. Next hairst maybe. Sandy Mair! Horse's Tail!

<u>1st Boy.</u> *(Disparagingly to Sandy)*

Dinna heed her. She's jist wintin us to chase her. She's gowkit. <u>To Helen.</u> Aye then Helen, we'll be ower tae your place the night, Helen, to tak a rise oot o auld Beanlie fan he's backing in yon bone shaker o his.

<u>Girl.</u> *(Still huffy)* Good night then, Helen.

<u>Boys reply.</u> Good riddance. Bella Buck Teeth!

<u>Sandy.</u> Ye'll be at the mill the morn, Helen?

<u>Helen.</u> Aye. I'm lowsin.

<u>Sandy.</u> Wi' Auld Beanlie?

<u>Helen.</u> Mhphhhm.

<u>Sandy.</u> (overcome with mirth) Look efter yersel then! Beanlie's an auld man but he's got twa three young ideas. He'll hae ye cowpit in o' the mill head first.

(Roars with laughter at his own mild ribaldry)

<u>Helen.</u> Nivir him! He never suppit the porridge for that!

More distant. Over shoulder as she has parted from group.

It's my last mill onywye. I'm startin work at Lendrum next week!

Boys. Various. Distant too.

See ye the nicht.

Tell Davy oor Dod's gaun tae gie him a han wi the sacks.

Jimmy here's jist gaun tae chase the field moosies!

Fade on their distant laughter

Country. Autumn sounds of early evening on their own. Whirr of a binder. Distant hum of harvest voices. Wood pigeons.

<u>Storyteller.</u>

Clova only found its own voice when its inhabitants had lost theirs. The sound of it rose awkward and incoherent. The whole sky became birds. Spreading clouds of them. Crows guttural in their geniality. Cushats which had lost their carefully modulated tones, their demure decorum, the instant they forsook their sober habitations in Carron Wood, for the slovenly world of brash birds, hovering on the stroke of a pinion, over the corn parks. Their music as far away now as morning itself. Their bickering begotten by the last great feast of the year.

Water effect.

The gossip of burns rushing down from Leuchar's Hill was endless. The corn added its ominous voice to the confusion of noise. Its hissing used to make the howe's days dim and drowsy; its nights alert and wakeful, but now it rustled with the harsh, dry rattle of death.

Solid things began to disappear. Insects clouded up from nowhere. A gauze of wings humming in a last panic. The mists began to steam thinly out from the seams of Leuchar's Hill. And the eyes that observed it sent the tidings round the howe.

<u>Country. 1st Man.</u> *(heard as in echo)* Aye faith. She'll be anither scorcher the morn.

2nd Man. *(replying in echo)*   Think ye that, then?

Fade

1st Woman. *(regretfully, as in echo also)*   The weather's gaun tae haud. A hale foreneens bakin for me at Mondynes the morn. The mill will be in efter a'.

Fade

2nd Woman. (Irritated to husband. Echoed also)   Helen hasna been fae Mondynes wi the milk yet. If they expect you tae gie them a han wi the mill the morn the least they could dae is tae send the milk in time for yer supper.

Her Boy.   She's on the road wi the milk. I saw her coming bye the station wi the scholars off the Lendrum train.

2nd Woman. *(Unappeased)* It's high time she won the length o the village then.

Fade

Storyteller. Even the village had taken on the voluble blowsiness of the surrounding Autumn. Its outlying cottages lay rooted in tansies. Straws drifting through it confirmed the current harvest.

Women claiked easily at their doors certain that the night had a lot of wear in it yet. Old Mrs Scobie too. I had thought she was dead. The quick vitality of the evening had resurrected her, and I resented such a resurrection. I hoped that she wouldn't notice me. I didn't want to speak to anybody at all. Certainly not to a ghost. . . .

Mrs Scobie. *(very old woman, breaking in on Storyteller's reflections. As if peering forward).* It's you, is it, Helen? Hoo is athing up bye wi ye a' at Mondynes? Yer Granfather's still tae the fore, they tell me?

(Chuckles gloatingly. To self, rather than to Helen)

Aye faith ye. Mondynes and me will see them a oot yet, a doon by the kirkyaird.

(Chuckles at the imagined triumph of this. Aware of, and to Helen now)

My, but you've fair shot up since I last laid een on ye. Ye was just a quinie the tither day. . .

Storyteller. I didn't want to speak to the old woman. I hated her, not fundamentally. But deeply. And at that instant. Speak to me. Speak to me. Her eyes implored. So that I will know I am still alive. I only know it when *other* folk think it.

Mrs Scobie. *(greedy to gossip.)* Ye'll be makin for Mrs Mudie's now then, will ye Helen? Poor sowl! She's nae keeping ower weel, they're saying. Something's gane rang in her heid like. They're makin oot that it's her time o life. She's gane clean off the Kirk, they say. And taen tae singin dirt o choruses instead, like orra Lendrum fowk at street corners. Her that was nae only Clova born, but Auld Kirk bred intae the bargain.

(Genuine bewilderment creeps into her voice)

There was neither time nor peety in my day for ailments that nae doctor could cure.

Fade

Children. *(Chanting their game. Faintly at first, increasing in volume to denote Storyteller's approach towards them.)*

> We planted an apple tree
> Over her head.
>
> Over her head.
> Over her head.

Fade slightly behind Storyteller.

<u>Storyteller.</u> Mrs Mudie's cottage was bereft of its familiar coterie of older children; always lured towards it by the fascinating rumour of its owner's madness. They could see a mad woman any day, but hairst came only once a year, and they had taken themselves to the fields, for the rare opportunity of teasing folk who were wise...

Children nearer.

> The apples grew ripe
> And they all fell down
> All fell down
> All fell down...

Fade slightly behind storyteller

<u>Storyteller</u> The younger children, unafraid and incurious, played outside her garden.

I entered Mrs Mudie's cottage with all the apprehension of Gretel entering the gingerbread house. Never quite certain whether witch or fairy godmother with a jeely piece, was in possession. Witch, tonight. Transforming Mrs Mudie into a tiger dimly pacing the cluttered kitchen. Blind to my entry and her evening milk, but wide eyed and beckoning to her own reflection in the over mantel mirror. Urging it shrilly.

> There is life for a look
> at the Crucified One
> There is life
> at this moment for thee.

The whole room throbbed to the quick, dark rhythm of its owner's mood. I was conscious of minute things happening. A fly climbing over a reel of cotton on the table. And aware of tremendous things taking place. The Grandfather clock panting the seconds over and past. The kettle curling on the hook. Hissing. Ready to spring. The dresser still but wary. The saucer eyes of its blue china, glinting and watchful.

<u>Storyteller as Helen.</u> Here's your night's milk, Mrs Mudie.

<u>Storyteller.</u> I spoke to the face reflection in the mirror. It seemed to be the realest face. It kept staring at its own origin, adjuring it shrilly

> Look, Sinner, Look
> Unto Him and be saved

I tried to put the milk pail down on the table very quietly. The table quivered with life too, and the milk pail shuddered in protest. Mrs Mudies went on singing, as I backed swiftly through her low doorway

> Unto Him who was nailed
> To the tree. . .

The village had lost all its own livingness since I had last looked at it, short seconds ago. Its houses stood as small and remote as the images of themselves for sale on postcards in Craig's shop in Summer. Or like dolls' houses. Craig's car a toy car, now. Craig himself a tiny tin man at its wheel.

But the boxwood in Mrs Mudie's garden shot up round my feet. Wild and pungent and bitter. A ladybird. Huge and red and clockwork, ticked and hummed across the bewildering boxwood in a blind, mechanical panic.

> Fly away home.
> Your house is on fire
> Your children all gone.

The sound of my own voice soothed me. The childishness of my words shamed me. No wonder Grandmother was always puzzling about what would happen to me when I. . . "got out in the world!" Here I was, almost going, and part of me still half believed that ladybirds could interpret and understand.

<u>Children   Various.</u>

> Was she wild, Helen?
> Has she got a gun?

Doddie Craig says she his. And she sheets a' the craws fan it's dark.

(Scornfully) She hasna got a gun at a'! I was aince inside there. She's jist got a bantam. And she gied me a piece.

Storyteller.   The normality of their words set my feet free now. Willing them to carry me out of Mrs Mudie's garden. Out through the village, thinning down into scattered crofts. Out towards Leuchar's Hill, slinking behind its own protective mists with each step that I took in its direction. I could have seen the whole of the world, if Leuchar's didn't rise, immense and blue, shutting Clova away from it all

Long ago, I used to think that if I ran very fast and hidden along the side of Carron Wood that I would catch up on Leuchars. Rush right into its foothills, and take it by surprise.

Evening.

Crofter. *(Hempriggs in greeting)* Weel, Helen. It's a rale fine nicht again!

Storyteller, *(who hasn't heard the greeting)*
But, no matter how fast I ran, how hidden my race was. No matter. Leuchar's Hill was ever swifter. Ever more wary. And I never caught up with it.

Crofter. *(Louder. Slightly intrigued)* I was saying that it's anither fine nicht again, Helen.

Storyteller. Hempriggs peered above his byre door. His eyes staring away into the fine nicht.

Crofter. Bit mebbe yer mind's nae on the weather at all, the noo, is it?

Helen. *(embarrassed)*   No. I was thinking aboot something else.

Crofter. Some chield or t'ither mebbe?

Helen. *(increased embarrassment)*   No. Nae that either. I – I was jist watching Leuchar's Hill.

Crofter. *(as if he has turned his eyes to the contemplation of Leuchar's Hill too. Not really believing Helen)*   Aye weel. Bit it's a gey hill, Leuchars. *(As if he has brought his eyes back to Helen's face again. Teasingly.)* So you're just no for letting on your thochts the nicht at a', Helen?

Helen. *(With awkward laughter)* No. Nae the nicht, Mr Tocher.

Storyteller. I laughed myself out of the reach of the crofter's curiosity, and into the safety of Carron Wood. Remembering suddenly that I had things to think about, important enough for telling after all.

Helen. *(shouts back)* I'm leaving Clova, Mr Tocher! I'm leaving next week. I'm starting work at Lendrum!

Storyteller. My shouts startled the wood. Set its cushats off on the scold. "We hear you" We hear you!" they confirmed grumblingly.

(wood sounds: wood pigeon)

I stood till the hot, scattered haze subsided, and the wood had gathered itself together again in still, dark concentration. Listening. Staring absorbed at its own reflection in Loch Manbeen below.

Two woods there always was on fine, mist-threatened nights like this. One stood high and sentinel over Clova, the other down and distant in the loch below.
> Two woods there was before ma een.
> But yin lies drowned
> In Loch Manbeen

The play of thoughts and words took me to the end of Carron Wood. To where it gave up its own large being with tortuous reluctance. And flung its remnants over Clova, in an unseeing frenzy. Its remnants rose in sullen copses. Dark and disconsolate.

(Intense sounds of evening wood. Curlew)

All else that was disconsolate in Clova found voice here too. A bereaved curlew wept its loss to earth. Some wild. unforgotten loss. "And Egypt!" a hidden bird called longingly.

<u>As Helen.</u> *(rushing down the slopes. To self really, but audible. Slightly excited)*

> And Egypt, And Egypt, and Egypt
> It cried.
> But never flew further
> Than Clova's hillside.

<u>Storyteller.</u> Unleashed by the desolation of Carron Wood now, I rushed downwards into the ordinary world again. Its large brightness bounded up to meet me. Its parks panted past me. Great wastes of gold.

Mondynes down in the hollow was the only solid thing in the whirling, sunlit world. It had gathered all its own within it. But the great sensation of light was just an illusion, after the dimness of Carron Wood, and the world settled down now. Dimming too.

<u>Male voice</u>. Down in the dimness now the heady rose
Turns black and humble with the coming eve.
And those fine Autumn blossoms spiked and close,
The marigold and the yellow zinnia weave
Their thick brocade.
Dreaming in the last moments of the sun. . .

<u>Uncle Davy.</u> *(shouting distant)* Ye'd better mak yer feet yer freens, Helen! *(nearer)* There's a gey bit steer gaun on downbye. Bad eneuch before, bit waur noo. *(Very near)* Yer Aunt Bell's swoopit doon on's fae Lendrum. . . .

Storyteller. Uncle Davy sloped across the dyke, like a shadow flung by one of the trees.

Davy. I made masel scarce. They hinna missed me doon bye yet. Bit they'll be beginning tae notice that you're ahint the nicht...

Storyteller. *(Laughter in voice)* The feckless ones. A knot of laughter broke inside me, wriggling through me in small smiles. The *useless* ones. That's us. That's me and my Uncle Davy. Weary Willie and Tired Tim. Ike and Moe.. All the funny folk I once knew in the comics. Leaning over a dyke in the dusk. Till the big, fat policeman moves us on...

Davy. *(intruding in thought. Severely)* I'll warrant ye've been on the dawdle again, Helen...

Storyteller. Uncle Davy unconsciously but severely withdrew himself from the comic strip. And Weary Willie had never been funny, left on his own. Aware of this, I volunteered very seriously...

As Helen. Hempriggs is gaun tae be scythin the inroads o' his barley the morn...

Davy. *(Alert. Interested)* Is he, by Cod? Did he mention it like?

Helen. No. Nae exactly. Bit I noticed. He had been sharpenin his scythe, And he was keeping his eye on the weather...

Storyteller. My Uncle Davy turned his eyes out towards the weather too. Leuchar's Hill was lost in the mist now. A flock of gulls traced a cloud in the sky. We watched them dipping and rising and borrowing strange colours from the sky.

Uncle Davy. *(As if watching)* That's the first o them flying inland. From the Broch likely. There'll be ithers tae follow. A storm at sea, I'll warrant. We'll land wi the tail end o't. Bit mebbe thae chieldies werna in flight when Hempriggs took his survey....

Helen. *(Knowing what will please Uncle Davy)* His barley's gey and thin. He's some gey rank like stuff in yon park o his.

Davy. *(Well pleased)* And sma winner at it. Hempriggs should have stuck till his concreting. He kens a lot aboot cement but deil all aboot the rotation of crops.

Storyteller. We contemplated our own barley. Still shaded with green here, by Carron, but yellow and mellowing thickly down rowards Hardhillock.

Uncle Davy. This wull be your last hairst wi's then, Helen.

Storyteller. It was just a statement. But somehow it compelled a reply. An expression of regret.

Helen. I'll miss ootside fan I go tae Lendrum. I'll miss ootside terribly.

Davy. Weel, I'm takin a taik up bye tae the heifers if onybody spiers. And ye'd best be makin tracks for the hoose, Helen. . . And tak nae heed o' yer Aunt Bella. She's jist a' tongue. *(more distant, twinkle in voice.)* Bit ye micht put up a prayer for yer Uncle Sandy. The sowl needs it. Haein tae bide wi yon targer!

Storyteller. The threshing mill flung its gaunt shadow across the corn park. The mill men shuffled within the radius of its shadow like ghost men. Grumbling, hollow sounds.

Male voices (various) *(Heard dimly, but distinctly)*

Roon wi her, Hugh.

Anither turn.

Roon wi her.

Roon yet.

Roon. Roon. Roon.

Storyteller. The voices of my younger brothers and sisters, condemned to play outwith the radius of the mill, leapt towards me, loud with life.

Children (various) *(distant, but approaching nearer)*

Helen! Aunt Bell's here fae Lendrum!

So's Uncle Sandy!

We canna get oor supper till they've haen theirs.

We winna get pease brose for supper in front o' Aunt Bell.

(Variously join in rhyme)

Pease brose , pease brose

Pease brose again, Mither!

Ye feed us a' like blackbirds

And that's a bloomin shame, Mither!

(They laugh, hugely amused by their daring)

We can go in noo, though!

We can go in wi Helen!

She's big. . . .

Storyteller. The "steer" that had possessed the kitchen all day, had subsided now, down into the quiet-after-supper moments. My uncle's long legs sprawled across the floor, hiding the linoleum. My grandfather's voice sprawled across the years. Other Autumns became tremendous on his tongue. Other hairsts became momentous. . . .

Grandfather. (old, but revitalised by reminiscences) . . . . Not a grain o corn stood up to the rain that year. Dingin on; hale watter.

Not a stook that was left stanin on its feet. By God, they were a sweemin! But ye could staun up there at the edge o Carron Wud, lookin ower Loch Manbeen tae Cladda yoner. Nivir a drop fell on it at a'. It aye pat me in mind o' yon hymn that Beanlie has sic a likin for –

Sweet fields beyond the swelling flood
Stand dressed in living green.

Grandmother. *(Breaking in swiftly and loudly. Glad of new distraction to cut Grandfather's old and oft repeated story short)* So ye won hame, Helen! High time tae! Your Aunt Bella's been waiting here for. . .

Storyteller. *(as if observing to self)* Grandmother's voice startled my uncle's long legs into their proper places. The floor lay clear and red and patterned. Grandfather's story sighed itself impatiently back into his memory. And Aunt Bella took over.

Aunt Bella. *(strident. "Towny". Given to gush and exaggeration)* Well. Well. So this is the Brood! A fine brood at that!

Storyteller. *(smiling)* My younger brothers and sisters, unused to Aunt Bella's exuberance, stared wide eyed and puzzled, as if she was referring to Grandmother's hens, and not to themselves at all. But Robbie and I took a sudden mutual interest in the rowan tree outside the window. Steeling ourselves against the giggles.

Aunt Bella. And this is no Sandy! Ye canna tell me that this is Sandy?

Storyteller. Our minds scornfully rejected Aunt Bella's assumed ignorance. But our eyes groped compelled over Sandy's face, reluctant to find him changed and transformed.

Aunt Bella And MY WORD! Hasn't Mary put on flesh?

Storyteller. I dreaded the moment when her eyes would light on me. I wished passionately that I could change into something big enough and strange enough to fit Aunt Bella's vision. . .

Aunt Bella. And hasn't Dod shot up. Mercy, what a size. . .

Storyteller If Dod turned into a giraffe right now, my thoughts raced, Aunt Bella would get such a shock that she couldn't utter another word. That would be right fine. The ridiculous thought got out of control, and spread itself grinningly across my face.

Aunt Bella. I just wadna have kent an <u>inch</u> of him if I'd met him on the road!

Male Voice. *(slightly amused, as if in whispered, conspiratorial tone in Helen's mind)*

> Of his bones are coral made
> Nothing of him doth fade
> But doth suffer a sea change
> Into something rich and strange.[1]

Storyteller. The words came to my rescue. . . .Into something rich and strange. . . My grin wrecked itself against the wide and wonderful phrase. . .

Aunt Bella. And HELEN! But of coorse, we'll be seein' a lot of Helen when she comes tae Lendrum. *(To Helen directly)* We'll mak a real Lendrum lady oot o' ye yet, Helen!

Grandmother. *(breaking in quickly, abruptly and irritatedly)* Ye'll hae nae need! She thinks she's that already! Lendrum! Lendrum! Lendrum! There's been naething else on her tongue this past week. And naething else in her heid either! *(As if looking up at the clock)* See'd'le the time! Half nine! That's Lendrum for ye! Taks her three hoors tae win the length o' the village and back wi' the milk noo! *(Still ostensibly to Aunt Bella but integrally to self. Puzzled.)* Queer thing aboot youngsters noo a days. They think Lendrum's the beginning and end o' the warld. Bit I nivir thocht tae gang farther than Clova for onything and athing life has tae offer in Lendrum. *(To Helen directly)* Ye micht cry the mill men in for their supper, Helen. Ye'll jist hae tae wait for yours noo till they're deen, lassie. An' see till't that Beanlie disna' cross my door without dichtin' his feet!

(Evening. Country sounds fade behind mill men, approaching for supper)

Mill Men. *(various, to Helen in passing, teasingly)*

So the brose is up, Helen?

Ye're gaun tae be lowsin till's the morn I hear?

Helen. Aye.

Mill Men. (various) Hear that, Beanlie? A fine young quine a' till yersel!

A change fae auld Maggie Hooch!

Naething wrang wi' auld Maggie Hooch.

Jist auld age!

(They laugh at this, over their shoulders to Helen as they recede from her)

Ye'll be fair itchin' wi' yavins this time the morn's nicht, Helen!

Ye ken the cure for that though?

Shak' yer sark afore the fire!

(They laugh tremendously at this advice.)

Storyteller. Leuchar's Hill lengthened in the ending day. Dusk brought it so near that it pressed down on the howe. Carron Wood stood silent now. Its trees rooted against the sky. A threat of wind began to tease the air. You could feel its latent devilry. Soon it would send the hill burn fuming down, and whirl the straws over the dykes. Bending the people darkly before it, like witches over all the howe. You suddenly realised why the Minister always prayed Guard us from the terrors of the night... Almost you wished for the wind to rise quickly, and blow the ominous moments sky high...

    <u>Male Voice</u>. Those lengthening moments
                  When the leaves are stirred, and night
                     Breaks with its wand the spell
                  That day has spun.
                  The damp, sweet mouths of field and forest clung.
                  The howe was still
                  The cheeping of the sparrows clicked and hung
                  Upon the muted rhythm of the air.
                  And, far off, with a small, disturbing cry
                  A voice assailed the redness of the sky.

    <u>Grandmother</u>. *(calling distant)* Helen! Helen!

Talks

The Cottar's Wife

When the BBC asked me if I would contribute to Farm Forum, I said: "Oh – I couldn't! I know nothing at all about the technical aspects of farming – the only thing I do know is what it is to be a farm worker's wife."

"That's the thing!" they said – "that'll do. Only try to make it general."

Well, that isn't very easy. I only fully know my own life, but I think if I portray it with truth, I must, in some measure, reflect the way of life of all the other farm workers' wives.

What struck me most when I first became a cottar-wife, twelve years ago, was that my neighbours' gardens bloomed fully and gaily with all kinds of annuals and bi-annuals . . . but never with apple trees! That was significant. In those days we hadn't enough security to plant apple trees . . .

Round about the middle of March we became restive; we'd hover about the doors in small groups, and the hoary joke that we shouted to each other over our gates had more apprehension than laughter in it . . . "Are ye workin' for bidin'?" . . . we'd cry to each other. For, by the end of March, a farm worker – and his wife! – knew their future fate. Either the farmer would sperr at us: "If we war thinkin' o' bidin' on for anither year?" . . or he would be ominously silent on the subject; his silence meant, that at the middle of May, we'd start "packing" . . and, at the end of May we'd hoist our bits of furniture on the top of a lorry, move off to some other farm, settle down – secure till next March came round; we'd "plant oot oor yairds" . . . but never with apple trees. They need time . . . and time was the one thing the cottar wife was never sure of!

One of the most important things in the cottar wife's life is her house. In twelve years I have had one decent, up-to-date house. Most of the others I've occupied defy description; in that you probably wouldn't believe me if I did attempt to describe them. It's fair to say that in one of them I knew my own rats; beautiful, fat, glossy creatures; they were so plentiful, and became so tame, that they lunched with my hens; hens and rats shared the same feeding trough; maybe the hens thought they were some sort of domesticated animals! . . . In another house half a ceiling collapsed during a white-washing operation, and most of the houses I've occupied have had this in common: they were dank and old, they had no modern conveniences, and they took the heart out of one to try and clean them.

In our district there is a scheme afoot; new, modern houses are being built for farm workers. The snag is: the rent of such a house is going to be thirty-six pounds a year; take an orra-man's wage – four pounds ten shillings per week.   By the time his milk, insurance and rent at the rate of fourteen shillings a week comes off that, he has about three pounds five to come and go on. Not very much considering the cost of living today.

One good and invaluable thing about this new housing scheme is that the house will belong to the farm worker as long as he pays the rent . . Whether he has a row with his grieve or gets sacked by his farmer. His house will no longer be tied to one particular farm.

The "tied house" was never to my mind a good thing. So very often groups of two or three cottar houses stand together in remote places. We women have to depend so often – solely on each other's company. Ask any cottar wife what she considers her greatest blessing, and she'll tell you, "A good neighbour". Ask her the greatest curse, and she'll tell you, "a bad one!". . . And this is a *fact*, where there are three cottar houses together, one of the three wives is always – to use a telling, doric phrase, an ootlin. And many farmers will back me up in this . . . the wives "rowing" cost them some of their best workers! . . . . . . This new, housing scheme will *not* stop us women having angry words with each other – no scheme ever invented, or yet to come – will stop that! – but it will help to abolish that truly tragic figure in cottar life, "the ootlin".

Now that I've got the "grumbles" off my chest, I'd like to say that the cottar way of life has its own unique satisfaction and contentment. The farmer is never really "The Boss" in the remote, aloof sense of the word, there is very often a bond between farmer and worker that isn't to be found in any other type of work.

We are *interested* in each other. When one of the cottar wives has a baby – as often we do have! – it's the farmer's wife who comes down with the bowl of hot broth for her, and with the first "gift penny" for the baby. And many a pair of the farmer's son's breeks haps the hurdies o' the cottar's loon!

If the tractor-man takes the flu' and is off work for a week, the farmer always does one of two things; either he rings up the local doctor and demands: . . . "When to blazes will Dod be able to start work again – and is it really the flu' he has . . It wadna just be a wee touch o' laziness, wad it?" or he comes down to ask for Dod, and makes quite sure that Dod's pay packet *won't* be less heavy because he's been a week off work. Can you imagine some big firm of building contractors phoning the doctor to ask about some Dod on his huge pay roll – who is a mason's labourer!

And it's not all one-sided, we farm workers are just as interested in the farmer! We are proud for him when his bull is sold for hundreds of guineas; we don't show it – oh no! – we're too dour, too like the earth we work with to be demonstrative. We'll say drily to each other, "A hunner guineas for a bull calf! . . . Och weel, it's in a safe pooch – *we* winna snuff ony o't!" And yet, inwardly, we're pleased about it; go into the local pub after the sale and you'll *hear* just how proud. "Aye," you'll hear our baillie-cattleman saying to the baillie from another farm; "Aye, min, ye can say fat ye like, bit ye canna breed the hunner guinea kind up at Northies; ye hinna't in ye!" . . .

And finally, our farmer knows our weaknesses and generally is tolerant about them. I think of a farmer who came "to fee" a servant whose ability to work he never doubted, but about whose honesty he wanted to make quite certain.

"Hiv ye ony hennies, min?" he asked of his prospective employee.

"Aye," was the answer, I hiv ane or twa."

"That's a' richt," said the farmer, "I'll gie ye a pucklie corn for yer hennies tae haud ye on fae risin' oot o' yer bed in the middle o' the nicht an' helpin' yersel!"

To return to the country pub; go in some Saturday night and you'll hear our husbands, the farm workers, you'll hear them over their pint of beer ploughing last Spring's furrows over again, re-thacking the stacks of ten harvests ago, re-feeding the bull that won the Reserve in 1928 . . . Their work is more to them than just a job – it's something bred out of all their generations.

We'll leave them, mentally re-thacking their stacks; such a wise, satisfying thing to do; for . .

I think how, when our seasons all are sealed
Shall come the unchanging harvest from the field. [1]

"Country Years 1930-1940"

The world, seen from our School playground, small and green. Widening only when an aeroplane passed. For, in 1930, an aeroplane was still novel enough to us in the country to bring ourselves – and our "Dominie", - rushing out of school to follow its flight.

"Out into the world." Or rather, out to work on a farm. A ninety hour week with ten shillings a week in payment. And a "Sunday off" once a month. And, of course, many unofficial "minutes off" at the Kirk brig, our point of contact with the outside world, for a servant who found time to read a paper, became feckless in her Mistress's eyes! Learning from other servants at the Kirk brig that the "Town" was the best place for a girl wanting to get on! You could get a Thursday afternoon off in town; better money too. They were keen on girls from the country. You got a better chance to meet more boys. And, had we heard the latest song they were singing in town? If we didn't know it soon we felt we'd be behind all the world! May Marnoch, a nurse maid there, had brought it back last weekend. The very latest. I slunk through the fields trying hard to remember it:

I could write a sonnet
About your Easter bonnet,
And the girl I'm taking to the Easter Parade...

...Marina hats; penetrating even into the country. Our favourite store rising to the occasion as always, and supplying them for sixpence! ..."The King's life is drawing peacefully towards its close" said the rarely used wireless in the parlour. "It is sad, for he seemed a good man," said the farmer's wife. Would I bring in the tea now? And we could use up the cake she had baked on Tuesday... The Royal Romance... my Mistress herself waxing sentimental about it over the butter churn; ... "He must be in love to give up a Throne"... ... It moved me. But only in relation to my own imminent marriage! Which, somehow, my Mistress viewed with much *less* sentiment:

"Ye're far ower young! Neither of you have got a penny to bless yersels with! Which reminds me, I'm thinking of giving you that brass bed in a present. It's not much to look at. But you need it!"

Then shut even more away from the world. Up in the remoteness of the hills. Where anybody's calf dying of "the Scour" became a *universal* loss…Where one crofter letting his oats "steam up" seemed like an intrusion on life there. It never became *real* or important till the Minister introduced it in his sermon. The Sunday he had gone "fair mad" in the pulpit about the bombing of the Abyssinians, taking as his text:

> Thine are we, David. And on Thy side, thou son of Jesse.. . . And twisting it right round into; Thine are we, Christ, And on Thy side, Thou son of God. Against that man, Mussolini, as far as we could make out, talking it over on the way back to the hill. But, I must admit, even more important to us personally was the new Road and Bridge construction beginning in the Isle of Skye. Work for years to come, and good money. So . . . Over the sea to Skye it was for us. .. ..

I think of those years as the years of contrast. . .... A woman cleaning her small byre with her bare hands; gleaming, modern brakes flashing past her. An excavator looming giant-like on the road, and beyond it, far out at sea, Murochie, the Postman, rowing the mail over to the Isle of Pabay.

And high up in my house on the moor, myself and my friends,, who were all young together, young enough to be foolishly brave, waited for Hitler's threats to become real . . .   Or dissolve, so that we could be up and doing, or settled down enough in our mind to enjoy our own lives in Skye. Somehow, young Rory, sitting in my most comfortable chair, made the tales of his ancestors . . ... "The Strong Men of Elgol", *dead* a hundred years, more alive than Hitler.

Reality came suddenly. Colin, sergeant from another war, recruiting for the L.D.V. Excited, like a horse who was put to pasture, and has now been called in an emergency to the plough again. Construction men returning to the danger of cities to find the comfort of their *real* homes. Reserve men being called up, mostly naval; my husband restive to join up with his old regiment. Myself thinking vaguely: "I wish I could have taken in a stock of sugar before it's all bought up." And feeling personally and selfishly angry about having to leave my house. I knew that never again while I lived, would I get a tall house on a moor, furnished down to a teaspoon, for five shillings a week. Not even that, sometimes, when the owner had partaken not wisely but well, up at Elgol, and rather than face the Aunt with whom he lived, would find his way to my house for a bed, saying earnestly: "And I will be taking no rent from you this week. No rent at all. I wouldn't take a penny of rent from my good host!"

All the young folk whom the war hadn't yet claimed came to "ceilidh" with me on my last night in Skye. War gave our parting an irrevocable feeling. We sang all our favourite songs far into the night:

> When Summer's on the mountain, and green the glen.
> And heather bells are greeting the sun, again.
> Towns of men forsaking, the road we will be taking
> To where out hearts are waiting. . . . Moun-i-an-Doun.

We gave it all we had. We knew that at least some of us singing in that room would *not* be taking the road back again.

Landmarks in Time

"We'll have to be ordering out winter coal soon," my husband warned me the other day. And, in some of the big stores now, counter spaces are already being cleared for Christmas Cards. My grocer's notice has been advising me for a long time to . . . . "Join Our Christmas Club Now!" And the final, most tangible forewarning of winter stood displayed in a Caterer's window. A Christmas cake. A canister of tea. A Christmas pudding. A tin of shortbread. And . . . . "Place Your Order Today!" . . . the placard commanded.

It was almost as if winter was racing up behind the vanishing heels of Summer, and there was no Autumn at all! I *did* see the season mentioned in a gown shop window. "New Autumn shades", it informed me. But that didn't really count! As far as my *wardrobe* is concerned, there are but two seasons in my "Dress" year, Summer and Winter. Our climate being what it is, I can quite successfully, as the fashion writers put it, "Ring the Changes!" between my two seasons!

But the *real* Autumn itself, is elusive in the town. You can catch a glimpse of it in the very early morning, - a fine, white hoar on the grass. You can smell it in the early evenings, burning and smoking. It passes with a whimper. Not with a *bang*, as country Autumns do.

There, in the country, Autumn is the climax of the whole year. One of the very few anticipations where the reality never disappoints. And you are never, *never* unaware of Autumn in the country.

Even its noises are distinctive. The corn which has rustled in the fields all summer, now begins to protest at its own heaviness, and groans and crackles and disturbs your sleep. The cries of the birds, because they are fewer now, become isolated. Particularly that of the whaup . . .the "peesie weep", as we call it. If Autumn *had* a voice, I think it would have the sad, plaintive cry of the peesie weep.

Not that Autumn is sad at the *beginning!* I always lived very close to woods. And I could have *sworn* that the trees . . . "put up a fight" . . . . for survival. Flaming, flaunting and furious! Defying pity. Throwing out a red challenge that struck your eyes from all airts. Battling against winter like a stubborn old woman who won't admit that . . .she's . . . . "past it!"

Nor does winter ever quite defeat a wood. You may be trampling through dead bracken, the colour of tarnished gold, but, if you follow the bracken to its source, very often beside water, - you will see a wonder. There, slim and green like fern, the new, young bracken is beginning to shoot up. "Lovely curse", was our name for bracken. Because it is indeed, both lovely, *and* a curse! A man could spend the whole of his life best over his scythe, cutting it down. And, when all's done, he has but cut down the beauty of it, for its roots grow and multiply – and come up in *double* strength to curse some *other* man's land, and lifetime!

And harvest itself. The fields loud with people. Even the farm dog senses either the excitement, or the field mice! The men on the binder flinging passing oaths at the boys trying to climb up behind the dangerous machine. The women waiting unhurried, - as country women always *do* seem to wait! – their men's tea cooling in jugs beside the corn stooks. The smell of their newly baked scones; and their "try out" of the first of the season's raspberry jam. I never could make jam successfully, myself – it either emerged as liquid or "candy". But how my children loved the concoctions that resulted from my attempts!

Nevertheless, Autumn, to me, becomes condensed and solidified in a childhood memory of "Berry Picking Time". First of all my intense envy of the neighbouring Gipsy children. For they took the road south to the great straths of Blairgowrie for berry picking. Our back garden seemed so small by comparison! More, I had always to whistle while picking the black currants to prove to my elders that I wasn't eating them all! The first "test" of the jam lying dark and tempting in a saucer. The fate of the world – and certainly *our* fates! – seemed to depend on whether the jam had "set" or not. For the grown ups were well "out of humour" if the jam didn't set to their liking! The squabble about which of us was going to get the dubious privilege of ending up with the berry pan. Dubious, because the one who had the pleasure of consuming the remnants of the jam, also, alas, got the job of washing and polishing the berry pan. I was never quite sure whether this was worth all the apprehension that had preceded it!

Autumn, in the country, is a . . . gradual . . . ingathering. A gathering of men at the gale end of their houses, sawing blocks of wood for winter. A lorry whizzing up the road to deliver drums of paraffin for the lamps which are just beginning to be needed now. Women chatting outside their doors taking advantage of the last of the "light" nights. Then, one evening you would look across the fields, and find them strangely empty. The cattle had gone to the byres. They were "in" for the winter. *That* was an irrevocable landmark in time. The *closing* of a season.

There was a song we were taught in school. If I can remember the words, they are worth repeating.

> Why should we sorrow
> That Summer's dazzling ray
> So soon shall pass away
> While we can borrow
> From Autumn's mellow light
> A scene more truly bright.
>
> Where'er the eye can wander
> The garden and the field
> A richer prospect yield.
> Earth seems to squander
> Her plenty on the sheaf
> Her gold on every leaf. [1]

I've made it! I'm very pleased. Because, do you know something? I've never seen those words again, nor heard it sung, since I left school – twenty-five years ago.

That was Autumn. *This* is Autumn too. But, alas and alack, I'm going to miss it. I have a feeling that *any* evening now, as I emerge from the tube station some horrid little boy – with *no* sense of time! – is going to hurl me right into Winter with his plea. . . . "A Penny For the Guy, Lady?"

Glossary

Brief glossary of words which may be hard to guess in context

alow	under
alowe	on fire
antrin	odd, strange
auld-farrant	old
breering	sprouting
byded	stayed
chiel	fellow
claik	gossip
cooried	nestled
darg	work
dreels	drills
dreesome	doleful
drookit	drenched
eident	busy, diligent
fashous	annoying
foostiness	staleness
glaured	muddy
glower	gaze intently
gowk	simpleton
greet	cry
hantle	a large number
hap	wrap
jook	duck
leadin'	carrying the harvest grain home
leuch	laughed
lowe	glow, fire
mools	soil

pucklie	a little
reeshle	shake, agitate
re-thacking	rethatching
rodden-tree	rowan tree
rucks	stacks
scaffie	refuse collector
scraggit, scraggy	straggling
siccar	safe, secure
skirlin	scream, screech
sliver	slaver
soutar	cobbler
speir	inquire, ask
steer	bustle, commotion
strauchtenin	straightening
swalk	strong, agile
targer	violent, quarrelsome person, especially a woman
tine	leave behind, lose
tint	lost
trigness	neatness
wyvin wire	knitting needle
yalla yitie	yellow hammer
yavins	the beard of barley or oats

Bibliography

Books by Jessie Kesson. All these in print from B&W Publishing:

The White Bird Passes, 1958
Glitter of Mica, 1963
Where the Apple Ripens, 1983
Another Time, Another Place, 1985
Somewhere Beyond: *A Jessie Kesson Companion*, edited and introduced by
    Isobel Murray, 2000

Biography
Jessie Kesson: Writing Her Life, by Isobel Murray, Canongate, Edinburgh
    2000

Criticism

Joy Hendry, 'Jessie Kesson Country' in *The Scots Magazine*, October 1989,
    pp 11-22

Hugh Macpherson, 'Scottish Writers: Jessie Kesson' in *Scottish Book-
    Collector 2,* Issue 8 1990/1 pp 22-5

Scottish Writers Talking 1:*George Mackay Brown, Jessie Kesson, Norman
    MacCaig, William McIlvanney, David Toulmin* Interviewed by Isobel
    Murray and Bob Tait, edited by Isobel Murray, Kennedy and Boyd,
    [East Linton 1996], Glasgow 2008

Andrew Monnickenden, "Beauty or Beast? Landscape in the Fiction
    of Jessie Kesson" in Susanne Hagemann, ed, *Studies in Scottish
    Fiction 1945 to the Present*, Frankfurt, 1996, pp. 109-123

Isobel Murray, 'Jessie Kesson: Writing Herself' in *Northern Visions*, ed
    David Hewitt. John Tuckwell, East Linton, 1997, pp 180-189.

Glenda Norquay, 'Borderlines: Jessie Kesson's *The White Bird Passes*'
    in Carol Anderson and Aileen Christianson, eds, *Scottish Women's
    Fiction: 1920s to 1960s: Journeys into Being*, East Linton, 2000, pp 147-
    157

Isobel Murray, 'A Far Cry from the Kailyard: Jessie Kesson's *Glitter of
    Mica*' in Anderson and Christianson, above, pp 147-157.

Glenda Norquay, 'Wantin' bodies: Female Sexuality and the Grotesque in the fiction of Lorna Moon and Jessie Kesson' in Susanne Hagemann, ed, *Terranglian Territories: Proceedings of the Seventh International Conference on the Literature of Region and Nation,* Frankfurt am main, 2000.

Isobel Murray, 'Introduction', *Where the Apple Ripens,* B&W Publishing, Edinburgh 2000

Isobel Murray, 'Nan Shepherd and Jessie Kesson: an Unlikely Friendship' in *Aberdeen University Review*, Autumn 2001, pp 136-144.

Isobel Murray, "The Time of Their Lives: Two of Jessie Kesson's Fictional Heroines" in *Études Écossaises*, Numero 9 2003-4

Isobel Murray, '*The White Bird Passes*: How Jessie Kesson Reached the Final Version' in *Scottish Studies Review*, ed. Margery Palmer McCulloch and Murray G H Pittock, vol 7 No 1 Spring 2006, pp 68-79

Notes

Introduction

1 In *The Scotsman*, 21/4/80.
2 *The Childhood* (1949), in *Somewhere Beyond* (2000), pp 53, 57.
3 See Elizabeth Adair, 'Some Memories of my 21 years of radio in the BBC Aberdeen', in *The Book of the Braemar Gathering and Scottish Annual*, Braemar, 1989, p61.
4 Further details in WBP   final version' in SSR date pages FIND

'Country Dweller's Year' Published in *The Scots Magazine*, January-December 1946.

1 Rose Macaulay (1881-1958) "Three Days", 1919
2 Charlotte Perkins Gilman (1860-1935) "Summer Joy", *In This Our World*, 1893
3 Walter De La Mare (1873-1956) "Silver", *Peacock* Pie, 1913.
4 Francis Brett Young (1884-1954) "February", *Poems 1916-18.* 1919
5 William Wordsworth (1770-1850) "To My Sister", *Lyrical Ballads,* 1798. The poem begins: "It is the first mild day of March,/ Each minute sweeter than before."
6 Rupert Brooke (1887-1915) "The Old Vicarage, Grantchester", *1914 and Other Poems*, 1915.
7 John Drinkwater (1882-1937) "The Midlands", in *Georgian Poetry 1916-18*. Kesson quotes this again at 18 and 19, omitting the most 'poetic' touches: here, the husbandman is not 'lissom', and in 19 she omits 'and there an owly wing/Brushes the night'. She must have had trouble finding more realistic farming scenes in poetry!
8 Samuel Taylor Coleridge (1772-1834) "The Rime of the Ancient Mariner", *Lyrical Ballads,* 1798
9 Quoted in Frances S Osgood (1811-1950) *The Poetry of Flowers* 1844
10 Red River Valley : American folksong and cowboy music standard.
11 Herbert Trench (1864-1923) "Who has seen the Wind?", *New Poems,* 1907
12 Gerald Massey (1828-1907) "My Lyrical Life" III, 1896
13 Essential Works Order: government order from 1943 stopped farmworkers moving jobs – "stand-still".
14 William Wordsworth (1770-1850), "The Solitary Reaper", *Lyrical Ballads,* 1789
15 Wilfred Gibson (1878-1962) "Lament" (1916) *Collected Poems* 1926

16 and 17   See J Oxenford, *Old English Ditties* (nd). Poem set to music by George Macfarren. This poem is also quoted at greater length in a broadcast talk, "Landmarks in Time", p000.

18 and 19   John Drinkwater, "The Midlands", See n 7.

20 Edward Shanks (1892-1953) "A Night-Piece" Georgian *Poetry 1918-19*

21 Adaptation of popular song: cf. Crimean War – "Wha' saw the Forty-Second?"

22 Percy Bysshe Shelley (1792-1822) "Ode to the West Wind": "O, Wind, / If Winter comes, can spring be far behind!"1819

23 John Freeman (1880-1929) "November Skies" Kesson omits 5 lines

24 Thomas Hardy (1840-1928), 'The Oxen' *Moments of Vision*, 1917.

25 Traditional Scottish song.

Poems

Seasons' Spell *North-East Review,* June 1944.
Dusk *The Scots Magazine* March 1945.
Abriachan Summer *The Scots Magazine* July 1946

Stories

Winter's Wid *North-East Review*, December 1944
The Flowering Currant *The Scots Magazine* July 1945
Contentment *North-East Review* March 1946
May Melody *Noth-East Review* May 1946
Pilgrimage *The Scots Magazine* June 1946

Radio plays

Apples Be Ripe Broadcast 30 September 1946, Scottish Home Service

1 Kesson's own poem 'Autumn Dyke', first printed *The Scots Magazine 1946*.

2 'loveliest of trees': A E Housman, *A Shropshire Lad*, 1887.

3 and 4 John Drinkwater's 'The Midlands', also quoted in CDY. 1919.

5 'Johnnie Sangster': traditional folk song.

6 Thomas Hardy, 'In the time of the Breaking of Nations', *Moments of Vision*, 1917.

Highland Spring Broadcast 23 March 1947, Scottish Home Service

1 and 2 Fiona Macleod, 'The Lament of Darthool' with changed place names. From 'Foam of the Past', *From the Hills of Dream*, 1902.

3   'The Valley of Pale Blue Flowers' misquoted from Fiona Macleod from 'Through the Ivory Gate', *From the Hills of Dream*, 1902.

Over Lendrum Broadcast 25 October 1957, Scottish Home Service

1   "Full Fathom Five", song from Shakespeare's The Tempest.

Radio Talks

The Cottar's Wife BBC Farm Forum, 12 May, 1949.
1   John Drinkwater's 'The Midlands' 1919, often quoted.

The Country Years 1930-1940 BBC Woman's Hour 24 June 1954.

Landmarks in Time BBC Woman's Hour 17 September 1957
1   See Country Dweller's Year Notes, 16 and 17.

Kesson at last in a 'scarlet goon' after her graduation at Aberdeen University in April 1987 (courtesy of John Macintosh/University of Aberdeen)